EROS IN HELL

CREDITS

EROS IN HELL
Sex, Blood And Madness In Japanese Cinema
by Jack Hunter
ISBN 1 871592 93 3
© Jack Hunter & contributors 1998
CREATION CINEMA COLLECTION, VOLUME 9
A periodical, review-based publication
■■■■■
First published 1998 by:
Creation Books International
© Creation Books 1998
Design/layout/typesetting:
PCP International
Cover illustration:
"Ai No Corrida"
A Butcherbest Production
■■■■■
Picture acknowledgements:
Mr Jun Hatakeyama at Image Forum, Tokyo; BFI Stills Dept; Danish Film Institute; Romain Slocombe; Screen Edge; Manga Entertainment; Blast Books; Heibonsha Ltd, Tokyo. All other stills as credited, or from the Jack Hunter Collection, by courtesy of the film distributors' publicity departments.
Contributions:
Chapter on "Ai No Corrida" copyright © Rosemary Hawley Jarman 1998.
Chapter on Underground Cinema written in conjunction with Johannes Schonherr.
Translations:
Koji Wakamatsu interview translated by Teru Arima and Romain Slocombe, copyright © Romain Slocombe 1998. Shojin Fukui interview translated by Junko Kikuchi, copyright © Romain Slocombe 1998. Takao Nakano interview translated by Takako Maezono at Anglo-Nippon Partnership, copyright © Romain Slocombe 1998. Additional translations by Kanako Shinkado, Takako Maezono.
■■■■■
British Library Cataloguing in Publication Data:
A catalogue record for this book is available from the British Library
■■■■■
Author's acknowledgements
Special thanks to: Kanako Shinkado and Romain Slocombe, without whose help this book could not have been written.
Thanks also to: Billy Chainsaw, David Flint, Jun Hatakeyama, Mark Hejnar, Rosemary Jarman, Junko Kikuchi, Richard King, Takako Maezono, Makoto Ohrui, Johannes Schonherr, Machiko Slocombe, Peter Sotos, Derek Woodgate, and Yutaka at ANP.
Dedicated to Simon Dwyer
■■■■■
Creation Books
"Popular books for popular people"

Eros In Hell is a book about sex and violence; it is about a cinematic zone where these primal impulses, each aware of its own complicity in the other's existence, collide and generate a delirium whose intensity is often virtually psychedelic in its effect upon the viewer.

Japanese censorship permits (virtually) anything *except* the depiction of genitalia. Doubtless by default, this stringency has nonetheless provided what Western cinema has suffered from lack of: boundaries. For many European directors the all-too-easy descent into hardcore pornography inevitably goes hand in hand with the negation of vision and creativity, as the depiction of close-up penetration becomes the sole function of their art. Extreme underground Japanese film-makers, denied this option, have had to double back upon their own imaginative resources to emulate both the hypnotic impact and total flesh experience that hardcore offers. The result is a vision of the realm of sex as Hell on earth or, conversely, Hell's confines as the human body and the madness which that mortal incarceration confers.

Of course, not all the great Japanese films revolve on the "exploitation" axis of sex and violence; the scope of this study precludes detailed examination of such experimental/revolutionary/arthouse works as Atsushi Yamatoya's **Hairy Pistol**, Kinji Fukasaku's **Black Lizard**, Nagisa Oshima's **Diary Of A Shinjuku Thief**, Akio Jissoji's **Mandala**, Toshio Matsumoto's **Funeral Procession Of Roses**, Shuji Terayama's **Throw Away Your Books And Go Out** or Masahiro Shinoda's **Double Suicide**. Yet most of the main films featured in this book transcend their "exploitation" roots to stand apart as stylish works of extreme imagination, intelligence and innovation which are more than equal to their counterparts in world cinema.

The main aim of this book is to investigate a body of cinema rarely, even in underground circles, viewed uncut in the West; it will, I hope, give at least a glimpse of the extraordinary realm to be found in the Japanese cinema of sex, blood and madness. There are also considerable footnotes from which the reader may hopefully glean a more general history of Japanese cinema, as well as a glimpse into the ways of Japanese culture. It is also my hope that the reader may be inspired not only to locate and view these films for himself, but also to delve further into this forbidden genre and even, perhaps, emerge with a fuller study.

—Jack Hunter

NB: All films in this study are referred to initially by their original Japanese title (where known), and thereafter by their English release/translation title, except when only/better known in the West in the Japanese (e.g. **Onibaba**, **Tetsuo**).

1 • PINK GENERATION
a brief history of japanese porno
005

2 • POP AVANT-GARDE VIOLENCE
the films of koji wakamatsu
033

3 • SADOMANIA
the joys of torture
065

4 • AI NO CORRIDA
in the realm of the senses
103

5 • ABNORMAL WARD
the secret cinema of hisayasu sato
121

6 • ULTRAVIOLENCE
sex, slaughter, sacrifice
143

7 • GARBAGE MAN
the wild world of takao nakano
167

8 • PUNK GENERATION
notes on the japanese underground
185

PINK GENERATION

快楽の構造に

A BRIEF HISTORY OF JAPANESE PORNO

PINKU EIGA ("pink film") was a term popularized by Japanese production companies to promote the line of sexploitation movies they developed in the 1960s to the early 1970s, "pink film" quickly becoming established as an equivalent term to the West's "blue movies". The first major pink film is generally considered to be **Hakujitsumu (Daydream**, 1964), directed by Tetsuji Takechi, who since became known as the "Godfather of Japanese porno cinema".[1] Produced by Shochiku Studios, this was the first of the so-called "Japanese New Wave" films to present a blatantly erotic storyline, featuring female nudity and even a brief glimpse of armpit and pubic hair, very much taboo in Japanese society.[2]

The "daydream" of the film's title is experienced by a young artist whilst under anaesthesia at his dentist's. He hallucinates about a pretty young girl whom he met in the waiting-room, seeing her subjected to all kinds of sexual molestation, rape and torture by the sadistic dentist. This includes hanging her from the ceiling and electric shock treatment. When he wakes up, the reality – or otherwise – of his voyeuristic experience becomes ambiguous. Guaranteed wide distribution by dint of deriving from a work by popular, respected novelist Junichiro Tanizaki[3], **Daydream** opened at the same time as the Tokyo Olympics, causing much embarrassment to the Japanese government, who strongly objected to the "amoral" image of their nation the film might give to the rest of the world.[4]

Takechi followed this with the even more controversial **Kuroi Yuki (Black Snow**, 1965),[5] a Nikkatsu production whose explosive mix of sex and politics finally proved too much provocation for the governmental censors. Takechi was arrested on charges of obscenity and sent to trial. The trial became a media event, with many participating intellectuals and artists defending the film director, as in

Tetsuji Takechi's **Daydream**

the Western cases against books like *Lady Chatterley* and *Last Exit To Brooklyn*. And as in those trials, the defendant won, shaming the repressive state and opening the floodgates for a new era of nudity and permissiveness.[6]

Seijun Suzuki's **Gate Of Flesh**

As a direct result of these events, a government-operated censorship board, Eirin (*Eiga Rinri Kitei Kanri Iinkai*), was set up in the mid-'60s. The major aim of this board was, it seemed, to regulate the appearance of pubic hair and/or genitalia in films, whether domestic or foreign. As opposed to the Western method of censorship – cutting – Eirin were content to optically disguise any offending areas, leaving the footage intact. Whether the viewer's resulting frustration is ultimately preferable to complete cutting – where, presumably, at least he doesn't know what he's missing – remains a moot point. Eirin did their job with little resistance or controversy until the '70s – when they clashed head on with Nikkatsu.

Nikkatsu was a Tokyo-based film production company operating from around 1954 onwards[7] in much the same way as Hammer Films was in England, using in-house production teams and resident studio directors to churn out populist/exploitative movies based on the trends of the day, from youth dramas, disaster movies, crime and adventure/romance through to the occasional rubber monster movie. Among the most notable *auteur* directors to graduate from the Nikkatsu system were Koji Wakamatsu [see chapter 2] and Seijun Suzuki, whose surrealistic *yakuza* (gangster) film **Koroshi No Rakuin (Branded To Kill**, 1967) – an elliptical avant-garde *noir* meditation on sex, violence and identity – is now regarded as being among the greatest of all Japanese movies.

Suzuki had produced around 40 films for Nikkatsu over a 10-year period. His previous films, which included **Yaju No Seishun (Wild Beast Of Youth**, 1963), **Nikutai No Mon (Gate Of Flesh**, 1964), **Kenka Ereji (Elegy To Violence**, 1965), and **Tokyo Nagaremono (Tokyo Drifter**, 1966),[8] had proved increasingly puzzling to both the mainstream press and mainstream audiences, and thus annoying to Kyusaku Hori, the President of Nikkatsu. When **Branded To Kill** opened to the worst critical mauling yet, and left most viewers totally bewildered, Hori responded by sacking Suzuki. Suzuki retaliated with a lawsuit, which was eventually settled out of court. However, his defiance was perceived as dishonorable by the other film studios and he was effectively blacklisted for the next decade. Nikkatsu also banned all his films from being screened, anywhere, for several years.

While many independent Western film companies had settled on the horror film as their staple money-earner by the early 1970s, Nikkatsu turned to another form of exploitation to achieve their greatest success: the "artistic" – but controversial – porno movie, marketed under the title *roman porno* (short for "romance pornography"). Their first so-called *roman porno* picture was Shogoro Nishimura's **Danchizuma Hirusagari No Joji (Apartment Wife: Affair In The Afternoon** *aka* **From Three To Sex,** 1971).[9] The plot, briefly summarized, concerns a woman whose husband cannot satisfy her sexually. She eventually takes a lover who can bring her to orgasm, but her affair is discovered by the madam of a brothel who subsequently blackmails her into working as one of her prostitutes. For the first time, sex was the *raison d'être* for a film, not just a by-product. This rather sordid erotic theme proved a great success, and Nikkatsu launched into a whole program of similar movies. It was just the start of a tidal wave of adult sexploitation which would flood Japan in the following years.

As before, the *roman porno* films were produced largely by studio teams and directors, who were given a free rein artistically so long as the films fitted a basic formua: a lurid, sensational title and an abundance of naked female flesh. The most prolific *roman porno* directors included Tatsumi Kumashiro (known as the "King of *roman porno*"), Akira Kato, Masaru Konuma, Shogoro Nishimura, Noboru Tanaka, Toru Murakawa, Toshiya Fujita, Kichitaro Negishi, and Yasuharu Hasebe. Their films are stylish, technically superb, and often feature impressive surrealistic touches. Amongst the 100s of films produced by them and others for Nikkatsu since 1971 are such gems as **Wet Lips, Ecstasy Of White Fingers, Night Of The She-Cats,** and Sayuri Ichijo's **Wet Lust** (1972); **Secret Chronicle: Prostitute Torture Hell, Female Hell: Wet Forest** and **Love Hunter: Hot Skin** (1973); **Filthy Virgin, Joy Street** and **Secret Chronicle: She-Beast Market** (1974); **Black Rose Rising** and **Wet Lust: Open Tulip** (1975); **Mad Love** and **Live Act: Top Stripper** (1976); **School Mistress** (1977); **Painful Bliss! Final Twist** (1978); **Woman With Red Hair** (1979); **Nurse's Journal: Nasty File** and **Wife's Sexual Fantasy: Before Husband's Eyes** (1980); **Do It Again Like An Animal, I Will Grope You,** and **Uniform Girls: The Fruit Is Ripe** (1981); **Let Me Die For Ten Seconds** (1982); **Double Bed** (1983); **White Uniform Story: Rape!** (1984); **Eve Is Getting Wet** (1985); and the women's prison epic **Women In Heat Behind Bars** (1987).

Nikkatsu also inaugurated whole series or mini-series of films with the same generic title or kink, milking them until their popularity waned and the next cycle commenced. These have included the **Love Hunter** trilogy (1973), the **Female Teacher** series (1977/83), the **Pink Curtain** trilogy (1983/84, about incest), and the voyeuristic **Zoom-Up** series (1981/86).[10]

In no time, porn actresses like Jun Miho, Naomi Tani, Yuki Minami, Hiroko Isayama, Moeko Ezawa, Yoko Hatanaka, Sayuri Ichijo, Junko Miyashita, Reiko Nakamura, Keiko Sekine, Rei Nakagawa, Akemi Nijo, Etsuko Hara and Mina Asami became national celebrities – symbols of a new sexual liberation.

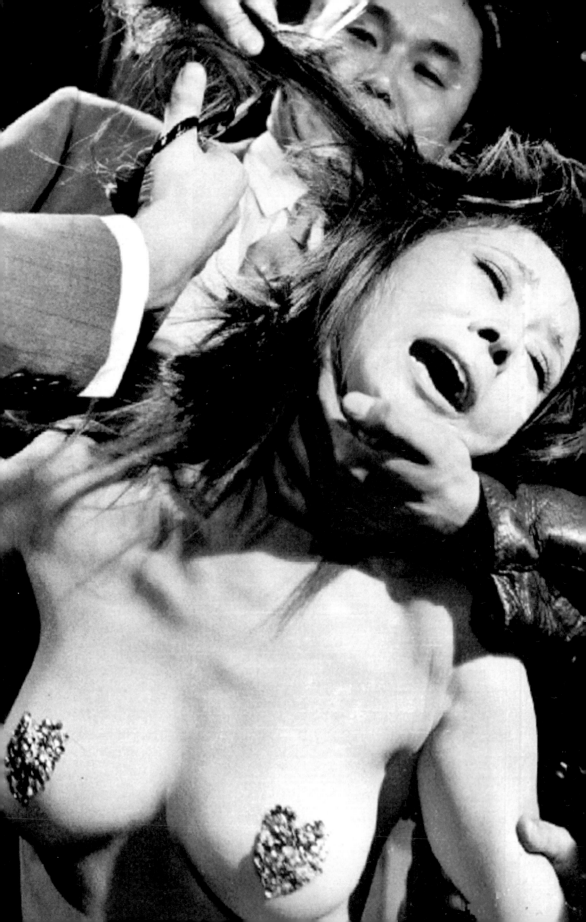

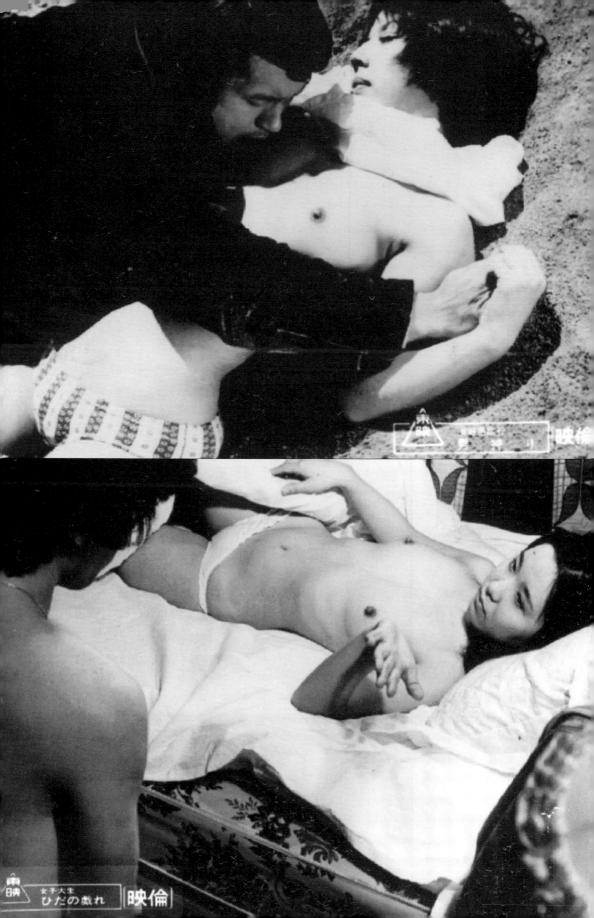

オールカラー さいはての情事 映倫 2

3 オールカラー 愛のテクニック 映倫

痴漢の指先 映倫

ーお捜みいたします 映倫

Another milestone in the evolution of *roman porno* came in 1973, with the release of Masaru Konuma's **Harusagari No Joji: Koto-Mandara (Afternoon Affair: Kyoto Holy Tapestry)**.[11] This was the first Nikkatsu film to integrate an overt S/M theme, paving the way for further, more extreme excursions into the sado-sexual arena which were also quickly emulated by rival production companies, hastening the mainstream acceptance of S/M in Japan. Among the most notable Nikkatsu *roman porno* movies with a distinct S/M tone are **Flower And Snake** and **Wife To Be Sacrificed** (1974), **Slave Wife** (1980), **Rope Slave** (1981)[12], **Fairy In A Cage** (1982), **Rope And Breasts** (1983), **Female Bondage Torture** (1984), **Beautiful Teacher In Torture Hell** and **Woman In The Box: Virgin Sacrifice** (1985), and **Erotic Seduction: Flesh Bondage** (1987). The main thrust of most of these works is confinement, bondage, cruelty, torture and even rape against women, themes which had festered in the sub-texts of Japanese cinema since the '60s and were ready to erupt in the subsequent two decades [see chapter 3].

The second significant event of 1973 for Nikkatsu related to another film, Seiichiro Yamaguchi's **Koi No Karyudo (Love Hunter)**. It was with this movie that the company finally fell foul of Eirin, who had apparently reached breaking-point regarding the company's continual stretching of the acceptable boundaries regarding wholesale nudity and sordid or perverted plotlines.[13] Director Yamaguchi was arrested for obscenity, but he protested vehemently and won over the media, who backed him during his trial. He was acquitted; yet again, the

filmmakers had triumphed over the attempted repressions of the censors. By the time such "hardcore"[14] Nikkatsu productions as **Uno Koichiro No Kangofu-ryo Nikki (Uno Koichiro's Nurses' Journal**, 1979) appeared, there was scant protest from officialdom. Though the practice of hazing genitalia persists to this day in both pink film and pornographic photography, there is now little – if anything – else which seems to attract much concern in Japanese society.[15]

Roman porno saved Nikkatsu, and some critics have suggested it may have even saved the entire Japanese film industry from imminent disaster. Certainly, these sophisticated movies proved a successful antidote to the undercurrents of sentimentality and banal melodrama often associated with the most mainstream Japanese productions. As works of pure cinema, they are long overdue recognition and re-examination.

Toshiki Satoh's **Tandem**

In the mid to late 1980s, the market for shot-on-video material had all but overwhelmed the pink film industry; the Adult Video (AV) explosion ensured that all tastes were catered for, and series like **Bombshell Fuck,** and the mass output of entrepreneurs such as Toru Muranishi, were there to be enjoyed in the home. By 1988, Nikkatsu had ceased feature film production and were concentrating on AV, still producing questionable S/M material such as **Dark Hair: Velvet Soul,** and **Tales Of Sacred Humiliation,** the latter a hardcore epic featuring a deranged, mutant hunchback on an ultraviolent nun-raping mission.[16] From the very inauguration of the *pinku eiga*, Nikkatsu have pushed continually to expand the limits of censorship. Their confrontational efforts have resulted in the establishing of the pink film as one of the most commercial genres in Japanese cinema, and along the way they opened doors for countless others to follow in their wake – from the crude early efforts of exploitation companies to more challenging modern pinks such as **Topaz** (*aka* **Tokyo Decadence,** Ryu Murakami, 1991), **Chikandensha: Hitozuma-hen Okusama Wa Chijo (Perverted Train Groper: Horny Married Woman** *aka* **Tandem,** Toshiki Satoh, 1994), or **Karura No Yume (The Dream Of Garuda,** Takahisa Zeke, 1994).

NOTES

1 • In fact, **Daydream** was just the first pink film to gain mass attention. The appellation "pink film" actually arose around 1962/3, of American derivation, and was applied to the low-budget, low-profile "stag" films being produced by the likes of Satoru Kobayashi, a veteran director of Shintoho Studios. Kobayashi's **Free Flesh Trade** (1962) and **Flesh Market** (1962) were among his last films, an early response to the serious fall in audience attendances suddenly being felt by the Japanese studios.

*Kon Ichikawa'a **Punishment Room** (1956)*

2 • In many ways, **Daydream** was the logical culmination of a growing trend for films with increasingly lurid, provocative titles and subject matter. This trend originated in the late '50s with *taiyozoku* ("teenage rebel") films such as **Taiyo No Kisetsu (Season Of Violence)**, **Shokei No Heya (Punishment Room)**, or **Kurutta Kajitsu (Crazed Fruit)**, and led to exploitationers like **Zekkai No Rajo (Naked Island)** and **Nihiki No Mesuinu (Night Ladies)**. By 1964, Shochiku Studios had already weighed in with Minoru Shibuya's **Monroe No Yo Na Onna (A Girl Like Monroe)** and **Shin Onna Onna Onna Monogatari (Girls, Girls, Girls)**, a mondo striptease film by Takeo Kurata and Katsuo Akutagawa. The same year, Nikkatsu produced three risqué films by Ko Nakahira: **Getsuyobi No Yuka (Yuka On Monday)**, **Ryojin Nikki (A Predator's Diary)**, and **Suna No Ue Shokubutsugun (Flowers In The Sand)**. **Daydream** was the film which finally delivered these titles' promise – or at least, it was the first widely-seen one to do so. The Japanese film industry would never be the same again.

3 • Junichiro Tanazaki was born Tokyo, 1886, and made his literary debut in 1910. His works are generally concerned with the power of women over men, and as such carry distinct sado-masochistic undertones. Other films adapted from Tanazaki include Kon

*Yasuzo Masumura's **Spider Girl***

Ichikawa's **Kagi (The Key**, 1959); Keigo Kimura's **Chijin No Ai (Idiot In Love**, 1960) and **Futen Rojin Nikki (Diary Of A Mad Old Man**, 1962); Yasuzo Masumura's **Manji (Passion** *aka* **Swastika**, 1964) and Irezumi (Spider Girl *aka* **Spirit Of Tattoo**, 1965); Kenji Misumi's **Oni No Sumu Yakata (Devil's Temple**, 1969); and Tatsumi Kumashiro's 1974 Nikkatsu *roman porno* production of **The Key**.

*Tatsumi Kumashiro's **The Key***

4 • Takechi would subsequently re-make **Daydream** twice. **Daydream** (1981) reprises the storyline of the original movie, but includes more graphic scenes of hardcore action (genital close-ups, penetration), and occasional gore. With or without these sequences, the second **Daydream** is a striking film; stylish, sexy and surreal, with a remarkable debut by actress Kyoko Aizome who, naked for most of the movie, looks phenomenal throughout. **Daydream 2** (also known as **Captured For Sex**, 1987) is the sleaziest version of all, climaxing with a veritable orgy of misogynistic torture, yet retaining an impressive oneiric lode.

The original **Daydream** was eventually distributed in America by exploitation filmmaker Joseph Green (director of **The Brain That Wouldn't Die**, 1959, USA), who shot and spliced in additional psychedelic dream sequences. Takechi's other erotic films include the "mondo" striptease movies **Women, Oh! Women** (1963) and **It's A Woman's World** (1964); **Kokeimu (Dream Of The Red Room**, 1964); a sexualized version of the traditional **Genji Monogatari (The Tale Of Genji**, 1966); and **Sengo Zankoku Monogatari (Cruel Post-War Stories**, 1968).

5 • **Black Snow** is the story of a psychotic youth, the son of a prostitute. He has a fetishistic fixation for guns, and is unable to achieve sexual intercourse without the stimulus of a loaded gun at his fingertips. Apart from the obvious psycho-sexual overtones, his mania is revealed to be rooted in hate against American soldiers, some of whom have abused his mother. The film ends with a cathartic (orgasmic) eruption as the youth shoots a GI and is in turn shot dead by military police. Takechi commented in court: "I admit there are many nude scenes in the film, but they are psychological nude scenes symbolizing the defencelessness of the Japanese people in the face of the American invasion."

Yoshishige Yoshida's **Eros + Massacre**

The notion of utilising ostensibly erotic films (often known as *eroductions*) as a vehicle for political comment was subsequently taken up by directors such as Koji Wakamatsu [see chapter 2], Shohei Imamura with **Jinruigaku Nyumon (Pornographers,** 1966), Susumu Hani with **Hatsukoi Jigokuhen (First Love Inferno**, 1968), Kaneto Shindo with **Kagero (Heatwave Island**, 1969), and Yoshishige Yoshida with **Eros + Gyakusatsu**

Seijun Suzuki's **Branded To Kill**

(Eros + Massacre, 1969). Until the rise in popularity of *eroductions*, this subversion of a populist formula had occurred largely in *yakuza* (gangster) movies such as Nagisa Oshima's **Ai To Kibo No Machi (A Town Of Love And Hope**, 1959) and Masahiro Shinoda's **Kawaita Hana (Pale Flower**, 1964).

6 • It has been estimated that by 1967/8, pink films accounted for half of all film production in Japan.

7 • The company was in fact originally founded back in 1912, under the name *Nippon Katsudo Shashin Kabushiki Kaisha* (Japan Cinematograph Company), and as such is the oldest film company in Japan. However, competition from such rival companies as Shochiku and Toho led to Nikkatsu's production arm being merged to form a new company, Daiei. Only Nikkatsu's chain of cinemas remained, but by 1954 they had accumulated enough capital to resume production.

8 • As well as **Gate Of Flesh**, Suzuki directed other proto-pink films such as **Shun-pu Den (Joy Girls)**, **Suppadaka No Toshigoro (Age Of Nakedness)** and **Subete Ga Kurutte Iru (Everything Is Crazy)**. But it is his cycle of experimental *yakuza* movies, with their increasingly *outré* stylizations, for which he is most critically regarded; **Branded To Kill**, the final release, suggests an unholy marriage of Robbe-Grillet, Robert Aldrich and Tex Avery, a grotesque reel of surrealistic fury in which all the players (and the audience?) are victims.

9 • Other releases included Toshiya Fujita's **Hachigatsu No Nureta Suna (Wet Sand In August,** which he reprised a year later as **Hachigatsu Wa Eros No Nioi [August: Scent Of Eros]).**

Wet Rope Confession

10 • Nikkatsu would also create disparate films around shared "buzzwords", for example the *nureta* ("wet") films such as **Wet Sand (1971), Wet Homecoming (1972), Wet Rope Confession, Lovers Are Wet (1973), Wet Bundle (1974), Wet Weekend (1979), Woman's Trail: Wet Path (1980), Shoot And Wet,** and **Up And Wet (1984).** Another popular Japanese obsession, reflected in Nikkatsu productions like **Kangofu Nikki: Waisetsu Na Karute (Nurses' Journal: Nasty File, 1980)** and **Hakui Monogatori: Okasu! (White Uniform Story: Rape!, 1984),** is the violation of nurses. This is part of an increasingly popular medical fetishism which includes nurse rape, enforced enemas and tying up with bandages. This particular fetish, in its Japanese context, has also been taken up by Western artists such as Trevor Brown and Romain Slocombe (in his collection *City Of The Broken Dolls* [Creation Books, 1997]. As Slocombe has observed, the Japanese flag itself, after all, resembles nothing so much as a blood-stained bandage). The ultimate nurse violation film remains Koji Wakamatsu's murderous **Okasareta Byakui (Violated Angels,** 1967) [see chapter 2].

11 • **Afternoon Affair: Kyoto Tapestry** concerns a doomed romance between a young financier and the daughter of one of his wealthy clients. Although they fall in love and wish to marry, it turns out that the girl is involved in an incestuous, sado-sexual affair with her father, a deranged artist. Masaru Konuma went on to specialize in this type of movie, directing other notable entries such as **Hana To Hebi (Flower And Snake,** 1974), **Ikenie Fujin (Wife To Be Sacrificed,** 1974), and the even more outrageous **Nawa To Chibusa (Rope And Breasts,** 1983).

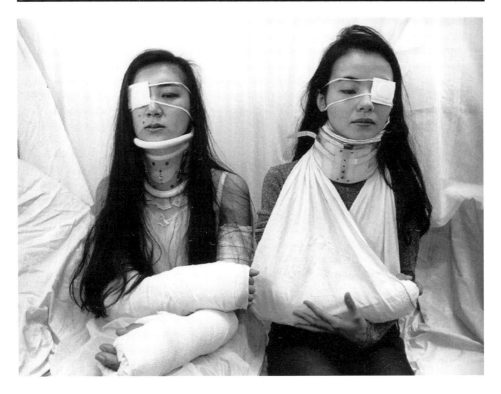

Medical art by Romain Slocombe

12 • **Rope Slave** features a screenplay by best-selling S/M novelist Oniroku Dan, as do **Fairy In A Cage** and **Beautiful Teacher In Torture Hell**. Dan previously wrote screenplays for the independent studio Dokuritsu. His book series *Flower And Snake* is notable for its fetishistic attention to detail in the description of bondage knots and techniques.

13 • Also confiscated and accused of obscenity were **Mesuneko No Nioi (Scent Of The Wildcat)** and **Shikijo Shimai (Erotic Sisters)**.

14 • "Hardcore" in the sense that penetration was obviously occurring on-screen – although the genital details would still be optically obscured by a blurred grid or mosaic. It is rumoured that at one time special glasses were developed, available on the black market, which counteract this "fogging".

15 • Walk into any sex shop in Shinjuku, Tokyo and you will find books and videos on paedophilia (known as *Roricon*, after Nabokov's *Lolita*), scatology, urolagnia, menstrual fetish, mutilation, bondage and rope torture, etc etc – but all with genitalia blacked out. Renowned photographer Nobuyoshi Araki – best known in the West for his collection *Tokyo Lucky Hole* – prefers to "censor" his own work with artistic ink swirls and blotches rather than submit to the standard governmental black circle. He has also been known to replace entire censored sex photos with images of graphic female mutilation – which are, of course, more acceptable.

Uncensored, "underground" videos and magazines *are* available, and are known as *uramedia*. These will contain full genital and penetration shots, fist-fucking, dildos etc. They are highly illegal but, because they are almost exclusively produced and controlled by the *yakuza* (Japanese mafia), police often turn a blind eye. In 1996

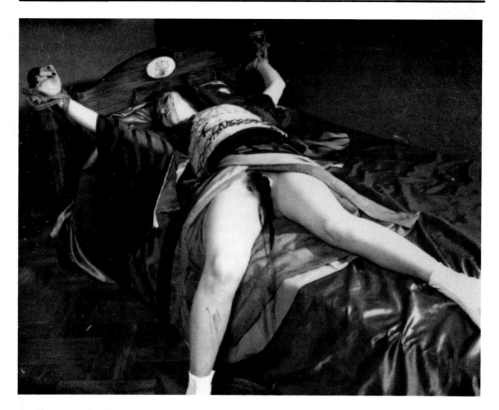

"Self-censored" photograph by Nobuyoshi Araki (© Araki, Heibonsha Ltd)

the laws regarding the depiction of genitalia were slightly relaxed, photographs of genitals now being legal – but only in a "non-erotic" context. Nonetheless Toshiharu Ikeda's 1998 version of Junichiro Tanazaki's **The Key** is reportedly the first mainstream Japanese film to feature full frontal nudity – possibly a case of history repeating itself, as a filmmaker uses the facade of Tanazaki's respectability to test the limits of censorship.

16 • Though maybe not as popular as nurse violation, nun violation occurs in several pink films, such as **Hiroku Onnadera (Secrets Of A Woman's Temple, 1969)**, Norifumi Suzuki's **Sei Ju Gakuen (Convent Of The Sacred Beast, 1974)** and **Dendo Baibaru Shisuta Gari (Electric Bible: Sister Hunting, 1992)**. Based on a *manga* (comic) strip by the director himself, Suzuki's **Sacred Beast** in particular is an outstanding film whose lush, saturated cinematography imparts surreal beauty to a clandestine world of lesbianism, bondage, flagellation, blasphemy, mutilation, murder, suicide and subterranean acid baths. Amongst many outstanding sequences is the pre-"Piss Christ" scene where a nun is stripped naked, chained, whipped and then force-fed gallons of water until her bladder erupts, submerging an effigy of Jesus in urine. Elsewhere, two topless nuns engage in a savage whip-fight, and later a nude nun is bound in barbed wire, whipped half to death and then showered in a storm of red rose petals. Suzuki directed several classily lurid sex films, including **Sentensei Inpu (Insatiable, 1971)** and **Dabide No Hoshi: Bishojo-gari (Star Of David: Beauty Hunting, 1979)** [see chapter 3].

POP AVANT-GARDE VIOLENCE

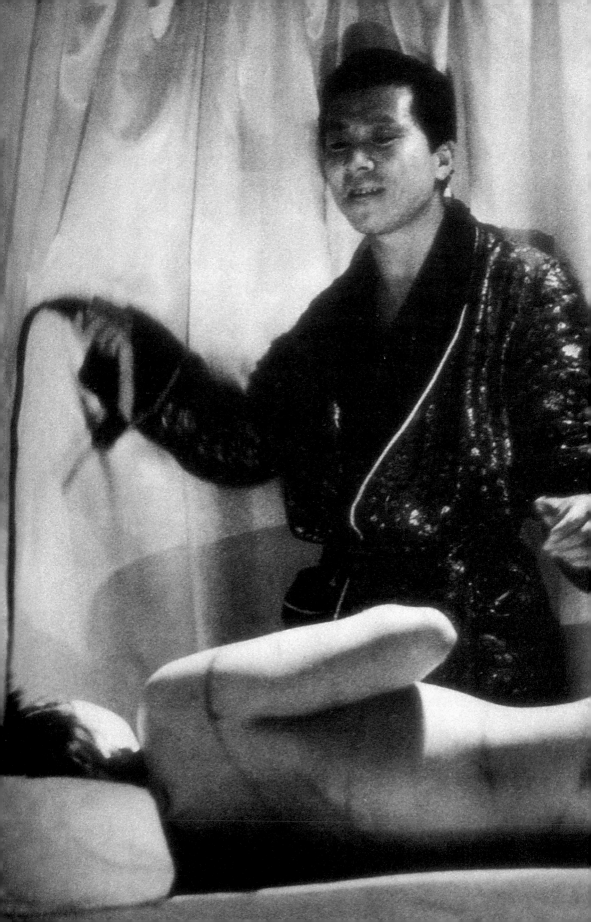

THE FILMS OF KOJI WAKAMATSU

若松孝二

BY the time Tetsuji Takechi's **Daydream** and **Black Snow** were released, Koji Wakamatsu had been a journeyman director at Nikkatsu for over two years, producing almost 20 films ranging in content from one flavour of the month to the next.[1] Evidently inspired by Takechi's revolutionary sex movies – and the "New Wave" films of his spiritual mentor, Nagisa Oshima[2] – Wakamatsu, like Seijun Suzuki before him, now decided to indulge these influences within the confines of a Nikkatsu production. The results would have profound repercussions on his career.

The film that Wakamatsu produced – **Kabe No Naka No Himegoto (Secret Acts Within Four Walls**, 1965) – was a radical departure.[3] The original project was supposed to be a film on middle-class students, the pressures of their lives as they prepare for important examinations[4], their social interactions etc. Wakamatsu hijacked the basic framework and filled it with a shocking psychodrama of scopophilia, rape and murder. In this new version, the protagonist is a teenaged student facing his college entrance exams in the knowledge that he is doomed to fail due to his previously poor education. Frustrated and maddened by his inadequacy in the eyes of society, he becomes a compulsive voyeur, masturbating as he spies on various women. One of the objects of his gaze is a rich, middle-class housewife who represents the very society which has scorned him, and which he hates with psychopathic intensity. He breaks into her house and brutally rapes her (despite – or perhaps because of – her willingness to fuck him). The woman is apparently so jaded, so numbed by her bourgeois existence that his assault barely seems to affect her; so the youth kills her, as he might have killed a sick animal.

Eirin, the censorship board, were plainly disturbed by this film and wavered over whether or not to pass it. Nikkatsu went ahead and submitted it to the Berlin Film Festival, despite government pleas to withold it – presumably for the same reasons they tried to hide **Daydream** from the Western world. At some point in the ensuing outcry, Nikkatsu apparently had a change of heart. Possibly fearful of a **Black Snow**-type prosecution, they opened the film for domestic

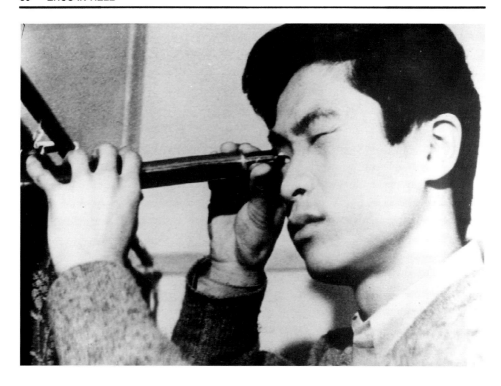

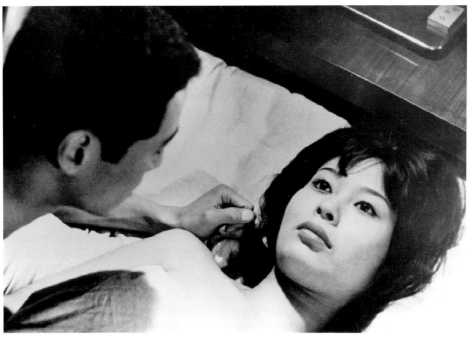

Secret Acts Within Four Walls

The Embryo Hunts In Secret

release with muted publicity. Wakamatsu, feeling that his studio had betrayed him by this *volte-face*, quit and went off to form his own film company, Wakamatsu Productions. A few months later he had already directed and produced his first independent movie.[5]

In **Secret Acts Within Four Walls**, Koji Wakamatsu had sown the seed of his "Cinema Psychotica", a seed which would flower spectacularly over the next few years with the release of such stunning, controversial works as **Taiji Ga Mitsuryo Suru Toki (The Embryo Hunts In Secret)**; **Okasareta Byakui (Violated Angels)**; **Yuke, Yuke, Nidome No Shojo (Go, Go, Second Time Virgin)**; and **Shojo Geba Geba (Geba Geba Virgin[6])**. These films at the core of Wakamatsu's Cinema Psychotica comprise a brutally experimental/primal apocalypse which easily transcends the limitations of exploitation yet still impacts with a visceral force unequalled by any comparable sequence in Western cinema.[7] At implosion point, Wakamatsu's films transgress into that zone of pure cinema inhabited by Bunuel's **Un Chien Andalou**, Kenneth Anger's **Inauguration Of The Pleasure Dome** and a handful of others, a zone where logocentric notions of narrative are immolated and infernal meta-texts combust in the right brain like neural napalm.

Upon the release of his first autonomous production **The Embryo Hunts In Secret** (1966)[8], Wakamatsu was quoted in the Western press as proclaiming: "For me, violence, the body and sex are an integral part of life"; as borne out by the film and its successors, this proved to be less an artistic defense than a genuine manifesto. Palpably still enraged by the adverse reaction to **Secret Acts**, Wakamatsu throws into **Embryo** every sexual psychosis, cinematic gut-punch and accompanying outrage his revolutionary imagination can spew forth.

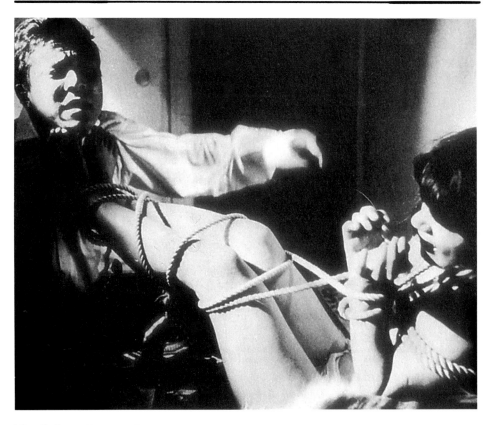

The Embryo Hunts In Secret

The "plot" of **Embryo** is simple; a disturbed man imprisons his girlfriend in his flat and subjects her to days of sadistic torture. But this simplicity is belied by the film's complex execution, its restless experimentation and fathomless undercurrents of spiritual anguish. Wakamatsu's **Embryo** is film as a physical weapon, a razor through the eye of the beholder.

The short title sequence – images of a foetus *in utero* set to choral music – instantly sets a tone of quasi-religious regression.[9] Cut to a rainswept night scene, a man making love to a girl in his car. Soon he takes her into his building, carries her upstairs, and they enter his apartment – and she enters a nightmare. The man's apartment is small (perhaps just two rooms), gloomy, oppressive – the typical Wakamatsu *mise-en-scène*, a static space in whose confines a psychosexual rite inexorably unfolds, inevitably leading to death.

The man undresses the girl, again we see him making love to her but already the tone is far from that of a conventional pink movie; the odd musical score, unflattering close-ups, raw camera movements suggest alienation, hatred. Before long he has tied her wrists together then, fetching a bullwhip from a closet, he proceeds to attack her in a vicious, prolonged flagellation sequence, his laughter suggesting sadistic glee in the assault, until she lies bloody and striped with livid welts on the floor. For the remainder of the film he subjects the girl to similar whip onslaughts, various types of bondage, and, most disturbingly, torture with a straight razor. These scenes of intense cruelty are intercut with flashbacks

The Embryo Hunts In Secret

in which the tormented man remembers his father abusing his mother in the same way; superimposed by images of religious martyrdom, the torture of women; and fragmented by Wakamatsu's trademark freezeframes, bleaches and still montages. Wakamatsu sculpts fear from the viscosity of the rooms, their mausoleum shadows and textures, and also utilises their structure to compartmentalise his screen space. The man's sadistic reveries give shape, organic form to the film's flux.

Typically, Wakamatsu inserts some scenes of perverse tenderness; the man brushing the girl's hair, applying her make-up even when she is bound, and later breaking down and weeping, curled up like the foetus of the film's title, head in her lap as she sings a haunting lullabye. But finally, the man's preordained death, the release he craves, is delivered. The girl cuts herself free of her bonds and, in a scene she has already fantasised, brutally and repeatedly stabs her captor to death. Our last glimpse of her is as she sits on the bed, traumatised, singing the lullabye to herself while the man's blood-spattered corpse reposes on the bedroom floor.

Chicago, July 13, 1966. Around midnight Corazon Amurao, a young nurse of Filipino origin, hears someone knocking on the door of her dormitory. She opens up sleepily, and a young pockmarked man strongly smelling of alcohol violently enters the house. It is 25-year-old Richard Speck, a man whose life has been determined by misogyny and sexual offences. Speck threatens the young female residents with a gun, ties them, and finally drags one after the other into an adjoining room. Muffled screams emanate as the deranged intruder brutally strangles or stabs his helpless victims. One of the nurses seems to remind him of his hated ex-wife (she was 15 when they married); he rapes her both vaginally and anally before mutilating her. All in all, the violator claims the lives of eight girls. Corazon Amurao alone survives the massacre hidden under a bed and identifies Speck later, above all because of the distinctive tattoo on his arm – "Born to raise Hell".[10]

Legend has it that Wakamatsu, inflamed by this provocative news story from the West, conceived and executed his extraordinary film **Violated Angels** (released in 1967) within a week of hearing about it. Apparently it was not the slaughter itself so much as the fact that one nurse survived, which appealed to Wakamatsu's sensibilities.[11]

Violated Angels opens with a series of still images, intercutting street scenes of the film's lead player, the actor/playwright Juro Kara[12], with nude women in provocative poses taken from commercial pornography. This establishes Kara's character as a disaffected individual with potentially unhealthy obsessions, an impression compounded by the first live-action scene, which shows him at night, discharging a handgun into the ocean. The immediate, obvious associations of gun as phallus and sea as maternal are deliberate and sustained powerfully throughout the remainder of Wakamatsu's hour-long, sado-sexual death trip. Like the torturer in **Embryo**, this is a dangerous young man: mother-fixated, impotent, only able to express himself sexually through violence. A man who seemingly wants to fuck, kill, annihilate all women.

Cut to a house where six student nurses are lodging. At the back of the house, two of the young girls are engaged in lesbian sex. Another nurse, who cannot sleep, sees them and rouses her friends. Soon all the girls – as well as we, the viewers – are spying on the naked couple and their lewd display. Then the young man with the pistol arrives at the house. One nurse sees him lurking outside, and innocently lets him in. For a while he joins in the voyeuristic game, watching the two nurses making love; but then, suddenly inflamed, he rushes into the room and shoots one of them dead at point-blank range.

From this moment on, the film becomes a fugue of claustrophobic ritual terror, the back room of the house an oneiric torture chamber from which we may not – dare not – avert our gaze. After this shocking assassination the five remaining nurses huddle together in terror. Wakamatsu's camera lingers sadistically on their sobbing faces, he captures their swelling hysteria by multi-tracking their mewling. The young man's sexual derangement is shown by visions of them in the nude. Finally one girl tries to escape, he guns her down. Another stands up and strips naked (close-ups of her breasts, his impassive face); she tries to make love to the boy, at first he is immobile but finally mounts her. Then he hesitates again – we assume due to impotence – and she starts to laugh at him. He imagines the others joining in the ridicule, their mocking laughter multi-tracked and distorted, their faces in swirling expressionistic close-ups, nude bodies superimposed. In the film's most explicit equation of the boy's gun to his phallus, he thrusts the barrel into the girl's vagina and pulls the trigger. A pattern of murderous gunfire (ejaculation), stasis, then psychotic arousal leading to further shooting is thus established, and persists throughout the film giving it the rhythmus of a bad wetdream.

Another girl starts to plead with the boy. All the while Wakamatsu's camera prowls about the charnel quarters, dwelling on the bloody corpses, sweeping back to the girl as she puts on her nurse's uniform. He ties her to a pillar, then uses a cut-throat razor to strip away the white cotton exposing her back and buttocks. Now follows perhaps the most harrowing sequence in the film,

Violated Angels

as the young psycho commences to slice her flesh to ribbons with the razor, virtually flaying her alive, casually whistling as he goes about his work. Close-ups of her tortured face are intercut with scenes of the ocean crashing ashore and the nude bodies of the remaining nurses, emphasising both the fantasy of maternal mutilation and the sexual ecstasy he derives during this hideously extended scene. Finally the girl's screaming subsides, and the young man unties the next nurse. He leads her over to inspect his handiwork, and Wakamatsu inserts a few seconds of colour as we view his last victim's ruined and blood-drenched body, her lifeless head wreathed in flowers. Hysterical, the untied girl tries to hide; the boy coldly shoots her once, twice, three times dead.

Now just one nurse survives. Surprisingly calm and impassive, she speaks gently to the boy, seeking to communicate with him while still in his "post-orgasmic" state. As he fondles her breasts she sings him a lullabye, he settles his head in her lap (in a direct reprise of a scene from **Embryo**); cut to a blue-tinted ocean scene, symbolising the maternal chord she seems to strike in the confused young killer. Wakamatsu now enters an extended colour sequence. We now see the two running naked along the shore as a couple, shots of sunrise, family, a montage of palliative imagery. On the soundtrack, a repetitive electronic treatment of the girl's lullabye.

Cut back to the house. The young nurse is now kneeling naked in the centre of the room, the boy curled in a foetal pose in front of her, also naked, head in her lap. The corpses of the slaughtered girls are arranged around them radially like the spokes of a pentagram, bright with blood, the damaged petals of a flesh flower. Wakamatsu surveys the carnage, then cuts to a shot of the boy

Violated Angels

as a happy child. When we cut back to the room, the nurse has vanished – the killer is alone, curled in the midst of the five murdered girls, the female death star he has smashed from its scorpionic axis. The colour segment ends. Next, armed police arrive, the frame freezing as they are about to smash down the door of the house with batons. Wakamatsu now alternates this suspended image with other still shots of rioting, protest, military action, revolution: a terminal elegy for youth/freedom.

It remains uncertain whether the nurse – the maternal archetype – has betrayed the boy and summoned the police, or whether she was in fact a figment of his imagination all along. Such details are perhaps irrelevant compared to the main thrust of **Violated Angels**, a work of primitive genius in which Wakamatsu reveals the ineluctable sexual pulse of the universe, and the cycles of birth, death, and rebirth that govern all matter. **Violated Angels** aligns this catamenial compulsion with the melancholy of the exposed embryo, the unbearable isolation in time and space that drives us to our daily rites of annihilation, and in doing so becomes perhaps the ultimate expression of Sadean cinema.[13]

1968 was a relatively unproductive year for Wakamatsu, as he only directed four movies[14]. But by 1969 he was back in full swing, with nine films to his credit including the bleak and violent **Go, Go, Second Time Virgin**.[15] This film focuses on two young, alienated protagonists, a boy and a girl, who have formed an

Go, Go, Second Time Virgin

uneasy relationship. As with many of his films, Wakamatsu sets the action in a bounded, single space – this time, the roof of a building. Our only reprieve from this environment comes via a series of flashbacks. The girl, it seems, is a perpetual rape victim; in the flashbacks we see her gang-raped by four youths, raped again by two of the youths, then raped by one of them assisted by his girlfriend. The boy has committed four bloody murders, which we again learn about in flashbacks. As in **Violated Angels**, Wakamatsu uses brief colour segments to display some of these gruesome scenes. It seems that the four adults he has killed include his parents; all four had been engaged in an orgy, during which the boy was himself molested. At one point, a woman urinates over him. His response is to stab them all.

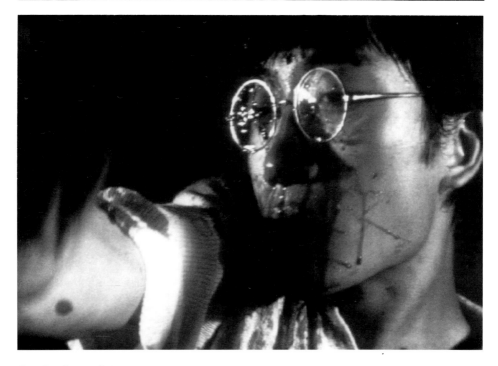

Go, Go, Second Time Virgin

More violence follows when the boy slaughters the four rapists (and their girlfriends). These scenes of violence are juxtaposed with almost lyrical passages, during which the boy and the girl cavort innocently on the rooftop accompanied by a poignant soundtrack. Night falls. Wakamatsu further compounds the air of confusion by now inserting a typical string of colour images – possibly representing the young couple's troubled dreams – both of commercial sex and violence and, more controversially, of Sharon Tate and Roman Polanski. Tate (eight months pregnant) had only recently been butchered in Los Angeles, and with this deliberate reference to a topical real-life crime, Wakamatsu repeats the correlation – also implicit in **Violated Angels** – of the malaise in contemporary society and his own configurations of sexual violence. At daybreak – traditionally a time for renewed optimism after the atavistic rigours of night – the young couple casually walk off the roof, plunging pointlessly to their deaths.

As explicitly as the Manson murders he evokes, as Altamont, as the drowning of Brian Jones, Wakamatsu's movie epitomises the auto-destruction of the "love generation" which marked 1969. But that same year Wakamatsu surpassed even the sexual derangement, carnage and morbid pessimism of **Go, Go, Second Time Virgin** with his masterpiece, **Shojo Geba Geba**.

Shojo Geba Geba is a stupendous 70-minute *tour-de-force* set in a desolate rural landscape which, it soon becomes apparent, represents an infernal circle of sex and violence from which there is no escape and in which all the pawns who play out Wakamatsu's cinematic schema are sentenced to either death or a purgatorial eternity as lost souls. As Wakamatsu himself has noted [see following interview], this *mise-en-scène* is just as claustrophobic as the nurses' dormitory in **Violated Angels**.[16]

The film opens in black and white with shots and freeze-frames of a night city set to a fractured percussive soundtrack, then cuts to two cars – one white, one black – speeding along the dirt roads of some bleak, deserted terrain. In the first car, three men hold a fourth, tied and blindfolded, captive. When they stop and pull the man out to urinate, the second car is shown to be full of jeering young women. Both cars then arrive at a barren, windswept spot marked by a huge wooden crucifix. A blindfolded woman is dragged from the second car and she and the blindfolded man are hurled into a gulley together. Despite his bonds, the man gropes the woman's crotch. The girls from the car, secretly watching, strip the couple semi-naked. The couple kiss, pondering their fate. We learn that the man, Hochi, works for a *yakuza* boss; he has made the mistake of having an affair with the boss's girlfriend, Hanako, and now they are both doomed to die. They are next stripped completely naked, as the girls continue their voyeuristic vigil.

Shojo Geba Geba

Finally the couple are pulled apart; Hanako, her blindfold removed, is lashed to the crucifix. Hochi is dragged up to look at her before being untied and shoved into a tent. Soon one of the girls enters the tent, strips naked and starts to make love to him, lasciviously pawing his body. Cut to the other girls jeering at Hanako on the cross. Cut back to the tent, where Hochi is now throttling the girl, strangling her to death. He slips beneath the back of the tent into the gulch and flees for his life. The thugs soon discover the girl's corpse and give chase to Hochi in their car, but he reaches terrain where they cannot follow. They give up, cursing him.

Shojo Geba Geba

Hochi flees into the distance, gasping and screaming in horror. We follow his flight for several miles, across barren tracts to the horizon. Here he collapses in exhaustion, and drifts into sleep haunted by Hanako calling his name. In a green-tinted sequence, soundless but for a musical track, he dreams of her being gang-raped by the thugs, next to the nude corpse of the strangled girl. She escapes, runs into the fields as the sequence erupts into full colour. Reunited, they make love, but as her hand caresses Hochi's back she suddenly feels an animal's tail growing from the base of his spine. Hochi wakes up abruptly.

For hours he wanders the wasteland, dressed only in the strangled girl's slip, tormented. Then, as daylight fades and the full fist of night balls into black, he encounters another group of people encamped on a hilltop. These men are dressed in fine suits and surrounded by naked concubines. Hochi is welcomed, fed, fondled by the girls. He is shown a rifle, mounted on a fixed tripod, with telescopic sights. Through the sights he sees a girl's breast and nipple, no more. They urge him to pull the trigger. He complies, firing a shot into the dark, and is rewarded by sex with both the whores.

In the morning the group are seen dressing, shaving, the girls exercising naked in the early sun. After they all pose for group photos by automatic camera, Hochi wanders off. Cut to him returning to the original site, greeted with unbridled hostility by the vicious, vengeful thugs. He ignores them, seeing only (in colour) Hanako, still slumped on the cross, with a bullet wound in her right breast. Blood is pouring the length of her body. She seems to be still alive. Hochi catches her blood in his cupped hands. Intercut with the thugs in black and white shots. Back to colour as Hochi realises it was *he* who shot her; it was *her* breast in the rifle sights. He drinks her blood as if in expiation. From this moment on Hochi seems to possess a messianic aura. His presence triggers mass psychosis, fear. We see him next in the tent, making necrophiliac advances to the strangled girl. The thugs strip their girlfriends naked, one by one, and shove them into the tent where Hochi brutally rapes them in turn as the dead girl "watches". Two of the girls flee and are pursued by two of the thugs. The third man sees Hanako stir on the cross and flees in atavistic terror.

Rifle shots. The men in suits pick off the fleeing girls and also open fire on the two remaining thugs, who head back to the crucifixion site. Cut to Hochi, who is now encased from head to toe in a sack, writhing like a crysalis behind the cross. Nude female corpses litter the ground around him. The thugs set upon him with baseball bats, beating him to an apparent pulp as the sack darkens with blood. Then, in homicidal frenzy, they set upon each other. One destroys the other's skull and then himself collapses dead. There are now corpses everywhere.

Hanako stirs, calls for Hochi. Miraculously still alive, he responds from the sack. A valedictory dialogue ensues, until Hanako finally expires from her wound. A bizarre ballad strikes up on the soundtrack.

Eventually the men in suits arrive, whores in tow. Gloating over the carnage of this nightmare Golgotha, they pose for more self-portraits in front of the crucified Hanako. Hochi silently emerges from the sack, baseball bat in hand. He has realised that the men are *yakuza*, and that the one who urged him to pull the trigger was in fact his boss – whose face he had never been allowed to see. In a quick series of freeze-frames showing the *yakuza* group posing in front of the cross, we see Hochi emerging behind them, ever nearer, his face a mask of twisted hate, until the screen erupts with the film's final, cathartic violence. Hochi brutally slays the entire group, girls included, finally dragging the boss to the foot of the crucifix where he caves in his skull like an eggshell.

A storm breaks. The field is now littered with bloody corpses. Return to colour for the final sequence. As the strange ballad once again strikes up, we see the cross in flames, as if blasted by lightning. Sporadic fires pock the terrain. Hochi bears his lover's body away through this blazing, apocalyptic landscape to vanishing-point.

In **Shojo Geba Geba** Wakamatsu employs customary devices – freeze-frames, white light, idiosyncratic soundtracking, jump cuts, colour segments to denote temporal, emotional or perspective shifts, and provocative widescreen compositions – to produce a cinema whose marriage of terse economic and virulent aesthetic has seldom been rivalled. Thematically, he clearly prefigures Pasolini's **Salo**,[17] both in his claustrophobic depictions of ineluctable, internecine sexual violence and in his implicit political assertion that beyond the law lies only an even deadlier noose of fascistic repression. In **Geba**, his psychosis finally achieves a truly religious intensity; Wakamatsu has produced the ultimate fusion of his terrifying, revolutionary obsessions.

By the release of **Shinjuku Mad** (1970), **Sex Jack** (1970) and **Tenshi No Kokotsu (The Angelic Orgasm**, 1972), the focus in Wakamatsu's movies had seemingly swung even more strongly from the pink to the political. Despite its title, **The Angelic Orgasm** contains a smaller ratio of sex to violence than many of its predecessors. The film follows the activities of an ultra-left-wing paramilitary group known as *Shikikyokai* ("Four Seasons Group"). The members of a sub-division called *Jugatsu* ("October") are assigned to rob an American military base, but the raid goes horribly wrong and four members are killed or maimed. The survivors realize a traitor has set them up, and rebel against the Group, forming their own radical troop dedicated to acts of random ultra-terrorism and sexual

Shinjuku Mad

Sex Jack

anarchy. They are eventually killed. By revealing that the October division were betrayed because of Group disapproval of their sexual mores, Wakamatsu again suggests that nihilistic acts of sex and violence are ultimately the only means of affirmation open to a young generation disowned by both mainstream Japanese society and its equally puritanical, repressive left-wing counterpart.[18]

Koji Wakamatsu must be viewed retrospectively as probably the greatest – and certainly most prolific, with over 100 films to date – underground/avant-garde film

The Angelic Orgasm

director Japan has ever produced. His outrageous, monomaniac films of the '60s helped pave the way for the public and governmental acceptance of sado-cinema enjoyed by more mainstream companies – including, ironically, his former employers Nikkatsu – in the '70s and '80s, while his relentless political motivation gives those films an undiminished subversive power. Recognition and rehabilitation for Wakamatsu as one of the leading forces in global cinema are long overdue.

Koji Wakamatsu was interviewed by Romain Slocombe at The Deep Gallery in Nogizaka, Tokyo, in February 1993. Also present were a lady Assistant of Wakamatsu, and an Editor from Eichi Publishing.

ROMAIN SLOCOMBE: Yesterday, in a bookshop of the Jinbocho quarter, I found a videocassette of one of your older films, **Yuke, Yuke, Nidome No Shojo.** I watched it this morning before coming here. The title is intriguing, but mainly I was surprised by the beauty of the images and of the jazz music. The story is rather simple, and the mood sort of intellectual, isn't it? This movie must have pleased the students of the time, the ones who liked films by Oshima. At the beginning, were your film more violent? Has there been a change in style?

KOJI WAKAMATSU: Yes. Between the 1960 Japan-America security treaty, and the 1970 one, the social situation became more and more tense. Student movements were getting increasingly violent. In parallel to this, my works became more and more eccentric. I shot this film on the roof terrace of the building where our office was. I shot it entirely on the roof! The idea came to me as I was breathing there, watching the sky! It hardly cost anything, just had to pay the crew and the

Go, Go, Second Time Virgin

actors. While shooting, I didn't know at all if it would turn into an interesting movie or not. It's the others who say if it's good or bad, etc. Myself, I don't understand anything about my films.

RS: During the shooting, do you often modify the script?

KW: I change it all the time.

RS: Still, you do have a script to begin from?

KW: Yes. Of course, one needs a script to prepare things, and inform the team.

RS: You didn't have too many problems concerning your relations with the producers, etc?

KW: Yes, they weren't happy at first because the finished film had nothing to do with the project I'd shown them before!

RS: Even a small production company like Art Theater Guild [ATG]?

KW: Yes. But what matters is to attract as many people as possible into the cinemas. After that, once they've realised it's a success, then they don't complain any more.

RS: The more *outré* the movie was, the more it attracted an audience?

KW: Yes, students mainly but not the general public. People in general would think my films were "dirty". My main audience was therefore an intellectual one, most of them being university students. On the other hand, quite a lot of poor workers from the Sanya ghetto would come.

RS: What was the average length of those films?

KW: Towards the beginning of my career, without thinking much, I always happened to make films lasting about 1 hour 20 minutes, and from time to time, 2 hours. And then, I began doing middle length films, about 1 hour. It's the case for **Okasareta Byakui**. When shooting that one, I had no intention of showing it in movie theatres. I wished to do a personal film. I was in the midst of shooting a more commercial one then, and I asked the actors to give me three more days in order to make **Okasareta Byakui**. And I phoned Juro Kara: "Hey, come and have fun with us!" I lured him by promising him two big prawns as a salary. Kara and I left the camera turning for three days, without thinking of anything. And it didn't cost much. I intended to show it in some small underground cinema. But it attracted attention from a few critics.

RS: Your films often deal with the relationship between a man and a woman, and you always show it (evolving) in a rather violent way. In an interview long ago, you said: "Between a man and a woman, there can be nothing but war." [Laughter]

KW: But yes, it's like war, their relationship! Actually the relation lasts longer when it's more tense and when there is a distance between two beings, don't you think so?

EDITOR: About **Yuke, Yuke, Nidome No Shojo**, Mr Wakamatsu, you said it had been shot entirely on the top of a building. In **Shojo Geba Geba**, you showed a cross erected in the middle of a desert. And **Okasareta Byakui** happens inside a closed, isolated room.

KW: I don't know why. But I enjoy creating a drama within a limited space. In this case, I regarded the desert as a locked room. It allows a concentration. Among my works, those which have been considered as successful were always shot inside an isolated room.

EDITOR: For you, Mr Slocombe, it is a hospital room, isn't it? You too feel attracted by the drama happening between a woman and a man shut up inside a room?

RS: Not exactly. Because in the case of my works, the man always stands outside the frame, one cannot see him, it is he who is the voyeur. For example, in a Japanese *bijin-ga* [woodblock print depicting a beautiful woman], we do not see the man contemplating her from outside the frame. And for me the image of the woman is enough. The spectator is left to wonder why this woman is injured, or bound. If I walk through a hospital corridor and pass by the closed doors of the rooms, I feel the desire of opening a door to discover what young woman is inside the room.

KW: I wonder if that desire doesn't come from your childhood. I feel you've kept until now that feeling you had while watching that broken doll you once mentioned, it's a feeling most people forget when they grow up. My film **Mizu No Nai Pool** [Pool Without Water, 1982] tried to revive this child's desire – practising cruel experiments on frogs, touching a doll in between the legs, acting as a voyeur, etc.

EDITOR: These truly are desires from childhood. Maybe you would have liked to dissect a woman's corpse?

RS: Mr Wakamatsu, I'd like to come back to **Yuke, Yuke, Nidome No Shojo**, which I just saw. I noticed the same purity in the hero of **Okasareta Byakui**, played by Juro Kara. He's had no sexual experience yet he feels both aggression and love towards women. And he can't make up his mind to kill that nurse, whom he recognizes to be as pure as himself. When the girl begs him not to rape her, their relationship remains pure. The hero of **Yuke, Yuke**... decides to kill the other, more adult, boys who have raped the woman. I got the impression that he himself wished to remain pure, and find a woman as pure as he.

Eros Eternal

KW: In the case of **Okasareta Byakui,** I was inspired by the nurse-killing by a young man in Chicago. The fact that one only girl hadn't been killed interested me. It seems that this girl was the only one to understand the boy's feelings, and that he just couldn't kill her. As for me, I am the youngest of seven brothers. We were all boys and we only had our mother. Spectators of my films often notice my Oedipus complex. I wonder if this personal tendency comes from my family situation during childhood. But apart from that, I feel admiration towards womanhood in general.

ASSISTANT: Or rather, a complex of the "Holy Virgin"?

KW: Exactly. I seek comfort in womanhood as in the Holy Mother, or in the Goddess Kannon [feminine incarnation of the Buddha of mercifulness].

RS: Precisely, I was able to see your film **Eros Eternal,** or **The Great Goddess Of Mercifulness** [Seibo Kannon Daibosatsu, 1977]. There too one finds this woman, who appears from the sea.

KW: Yes. I admit to be a big admirer of woman, if I reflect on the subject. For me a woman is a being who understands me and accepts me totally without me needing to explain myself. In my films one always finds a yearning for a woman of infinite grace and kindness.

RS: This is perhaps a very Japanese theme?

KW: Yes. It certainly comes from the surroundings and situation during my childhood.

EDITOR: There must exist some gap between that idealised woman, and those of the real world...

KW: Yes, of course. There are plenty of differences. But I prefer to continue seeking this ideal, rather than live in resignation.

EDITOR: For Romain Slocombe, this idealised woman is represented in these pictures of women wearing bandages, am I right?

KW: I understand this perfectly. The injured woman who can't move from her hospital bed, is in a way isolated from the real world: it's in such an unintentional immobility that she gives off more eroticism than in her normal state. I find a woman more erotic while she's asleep. In sleep, deprived of will, a woman exposes herself without wariness, without artifice. A naked woman sleeping is very beautiful sight. Actually I feel a lot of attraction when seeing a woman with bandages on a hospital bed. But if it's a sick woman, then she's much less erotic! [Laughter]

RS: True. The vision of a woman who's ill, calls to mind the eventuality of her death, and this is disagreeable to me. The woman bandaged or in a cast, can be apart from this in perfect health but has to bear it for a month or so, a motionless position. I find her more thrilling so.

EDITOR: Visually, white bandage is very beautiful. Mr Slocombe, you mentioned the purity of the hero of **Yuke, Yuke...**; it's purity which brings the hero to his death, isn't it? Mr Wakamatsu, why does your hero die at the end?

KW: ...That's because I thought it was a more stylish resolution. For example, I find Che Guevara very chic – I would have liked to live and die like him! Unfortunately, I'm going to end as a mere film director. That's why I went as far as Palestine to shoot a film. Following the principles of the film, the hero shouldn't die. But I thought it would be a finer ending if he died.

EDITOR: I believe the hero had to die in order to preserve his purity.

KW: I wasn't conscious of it. Because I don't use my brain much to do a film. I only respect my feelings and my sensitivity. And very often, actors don't understand what I want. I find myself very instinctive, like an animal. Never been to a cinema school, never learnt the cinematographic technique. It's by chance that I entered this profession. I had never dreamed of it! Simply, I had the urge to create something, either a text, either a film, by any means. I wished my desires to come true, for example the desire to kill cops! [Laughter] I cannot do this in real life, of course. But in a film I can exterminate a huge number of cops all at once. There you are, I started making movies for a very crude motive. Because of those first films, which met with some success, people began calling me a film director. Since then I shoot constantly, even today when conditions are more and more difficult. I do not construct a film inside my brain. The desire comes to me all of a sudden. For example, **Taiji Ga Mitsuryo Suru Toki** is born from an image I saw from the window, a rainy morning in May. First, there was an image. Then to this initial image I add other images, one by one. That's how I build a film, just with images. As soon as I've found this core-image, I summon the crew and the actors. If I'd had to wait a month or so, the desire would be gone already. It's always a nuisance when I'm asked: "That image there, what is it supposed to mean?"

RS: Did you conceive in the same way **Terroru No Kisetsu [Season Of Terror, 1969]**? The hero, who lives with two women, goes to blow up Haneda Airport at the end.

KW: Yes, I really knew this guy who lived with two women. Those two women had children almost at the same time. And they loved each other, they were lesbians! And all of them got on very well together. I found the situation very amusing and wanted to make a movie about those three people. It's only after that I added the detail of the man being a terrorist.

RS: Sex and terrorism, both themes were mixed together. For such a reason one

Season Of Terror

Sex Jack

of my books got censored in France.

KW: My film **Sex Jack** got banned in France too. It was first shown at Cannes festival, then forbidden – although some film fans had liked it. The problem was that at the end of the film, a "nice" young terrorist tries to kill the Prime Minister, They thought it was anti-social. As for **Okasareta Byakui**, they said there was too much blood.

RS: This intrigues me: in France or in England, a film or a comic showing S/M and violence towards women, faces censorship. While the depiction of sex scenes is widely tolerated. In Japan it's the reverse situation isn't it?

Shinjuku Mad

KW: Yes, to show S/M and violence in a film is perfectly OK. But for love scenes, some limits have been fixed. Which means one can't show everything, you understand? At European film festivals, people often laugh at Japanese movies, because the camera makes bizarre motions not to show certain things. I feel sort of embarrassed each time a European asks me: "What is the meaning of that rather brutal camera movement?" Why must one hide sexual organs? I believe that in Japan sex is the privilege of men who have power, like politicians, very rich people, etc. They all have girlfriends, don't they? In the past we Japanese were told: "You the poor people, be content with eating rice." And even now they say to us: "Be content without seeing images of sex." In the Edo period everything was more broad-minded, from what I heard. It is after the Meiji and Taisho periods that the authorities became very strict.

EDITOR: While S/M and violence still remained tolerated, as always in Japan.

KW: Yes. Perhaps because authorities believe these things to be absolutely normal.

EDITOR: I find that idea interesting, power monopolizing sex.

KW: That's why in my films I enjoy making fun of power, by associating it with sex.

RS: Have you noticed any recent changes, watching the work of young film-makers? Do you intend to try other styles of film?

KW: I often note that young directors show naked women in a solely commercial purpose. I find them quite superficial. That's why I rarely see their movies. My director friends and I, if we made *pinku eiga*, it was to express some kind of serious feeling. As for other film styles, I'd say I've already tried them all.

EDITOR: So, if I understood you right, even in your *pinku eiga*, the main subject wasn't sex.

KW: Right. First, at the time, I wasn't accepted by big production companies. To make a movie, I was forced to work in the field of *pinku eiga*. And my films had to be seen by the largest audience possible, so I put some rather scandalous titles to attract a greater public, like **Yuke, Yuke, Nidome No Shojo**. Reading the word "virgin", people imagine pornographic things and rush into the cinemas. What's important is that they are happy with what they saw, even if it wasn't at all what they expected, don't you think?

ASSISTANT: So now you can direct the movies you want to, they don't have to be *pinku eiga*?

KW: Yes, the situation has changed completely. I'm even currently shooting a film for TV. [Laughter]

NOTES

1 • Born 1936 in Miyagi Prefecture, Wakamatsu dropped out of Agricultural College in second grade, came to Tokyo and went through a succession of jobs including apprentice craftsman, delivery boy, and would-be gangster with the Shinjuku-based "Yasuda-gumi" mob – the latter activity landing him a spell in prison. Released at the age of 23, he finally became an assistant director for TV films, and in 1963 broke into cinema by directing a proto-pink movie called **Amai-Wana (Sweet Trap)**. He soon became renowned as a pulp director, his projects already distinguished by vivid and violent scenes. These early films include **Hageshii Onnatachi (Savage Women, 1963)**, **Mesuinu No Kake (The Games Of Bitches, 1964)**, **Hadaka No Kage (The Naked Shadow, 1964)**, and **Akai Hanko (Red Crime, 1964)**. In **Red Crime**, the chaste wife of a public attorney is raped by an escaped convict, and the film shows in detail the sexual relations between the three protagonists. Here we can already trace the seminal motifs of Wakamatsu's cinema: hatred, disgust for authority, and an Oedipal desire to re-enter the womb.

2 • Born in Kyoto, 1932, Nagisa Oshima was a graduate in Marxist history before joining Shochiku as an assistant director and scriptwriter in 1954. His first film as director was **Ai To Kibo No Machi (Town Of Love And Hope, 1959)**, followed by **Seishun Zankoku Monogatari (Cruel Story Of Youth, 1960)** and **Taiyo No Hakaba (The Sun's Burial, 1960)**. Inspired by Jean-Luc Godard, these films focused on youth crime and abusive relationships to comment on the state of contemporary Japan. **Nihon No Yoru To Kiri (Night And Fog In Japan, 1960)** was withdrawn by Shochiku due to its politically sensitive nature, prompting Oshima to quit the studio and direct **Shiiku (The Catch, 1961)** and **Amakusa Shiro Tokisada (The Rebel, 1962)** independently. He then formed his own production company, Sozosha, and worked in television for three years before going on to make such films as **Etsuraku (Pleasures Of The Flesh, 1965)**, **Hakuchu No Torima (Violence At Noon, 1966)**, **Koshikei (Death By Hanging, 1968)**, **Shinjuku Dorobo Nikki (Diary Of A Shinjuku Thief, 1968)**, **Shonen (Boy, 1969)** and **Gishiki (The Ceremony, 1971)**.

Nagisa Oshima's **The Ceremony**

Throughout this body of work – which established him firmly as the leader of Japanese cinema's "New Wave" – Oshima largely rejects conventional modes of narrative and uses the cinematic medium to promote his own political analysis of Japan. In the 1970s he finally quit the country, making the seminal **Ai No Koriida (1976)** [see chapter 4] as a French co-production. This was followed by other foreign collaborations including **Ai No Borei (Empire Of Passion, 1978)**, and **Merry Christmas Mr. Lawrence (1983)**.

3 • Wakamatsu's other films of 1965 include **Botoku No Wana (Filthy Trap)**, **Ai No Design (The Love Robots)** and **Joji No Rirekisho (Career Of Lust)** – the latter once described as the most successful of all pink movies.

4 • Japan has always had a notoriously high level of student suicides, due to the intense pressure to succeed.

5 • As a producer Wakamatsu was responsible for discovering directors such as Masao Adachi (**Seiyugi [Sex Games, 1968]**, **Ryakusho Renzoku Shasatsuma [A.K.A. Serial Killer, 1969]**, **Jogakusei Gerira [Schoolgirl Guerilla, 1969]**), and Atsushi Jiku Yamatoya (**Uragiri No Kisetsu [Season Of Treason, 1967]**, **Koya No Dacchi Waifu [Inflatable Sex Doll Of The Wastelands, 1967]**. He also produced Tatsumi Kumashiro's acclaimed **Akai Kami No Onna (Woman With Red Hair, 1979**, starring "Queen of Eros" Junko Miyashita), and was an executive producer of Nagisa Oshima's **Ai No Koriida** [see chapter 4].

6 • "Geba" has no literal translation. It derives from the German "gewalt", meaning strength or power, and is a political term used by leftist Japanese students to describe their movement (e.g. *geba-bo* ["staffs of power"], the long sticks used in violent encounters with police). A phonetic spelling of "gay bar" has also been posited as the word's meaning in **Shojo Geba Geba**'s title; since the title was reportedly suggested to Wakamatsu by Nagisa Oshima, a political connotation seems much more likely. For Wakamatsu's 1998 retrospective in Tokyo, the film was shown under the English title **Violent Virgin**.

7 • It is in fact estimated that between the inauguration of Wakamatsu Productions in 1965, and 1972, Wakamatsu produced around 45 films – mostly shot on ultra-low budgets equivalent to around $5,000, with an average turnaround of 16 days. Many of these have rarely, if ever, been seen in the West. The films discussed in this chapter are therefore not strictly sequential. Probably their nearest equivalent – in terms of singularity of vision, unflinching juxtaposition of sex and violence, visual poetry and psychotropic editing – would be Russ Meyer's quartet **Lorna (1964)**, **Mudhoney (1965)**, **Motorpsycho! (1965)**, and **Faster, Pussycat! Kill! Kill! (1966)**. Wakamatsu finally compounds all these elements with the political/experimental edge of a Jean-Luc Godard (minus the tedium) to create a devastating cinematic experience.

8 • Other films directed by Wakamatsu in 1966 include **Joyoku No Kurozuisen (Narcissus Of Lust)**, **Chi Wa Taiyo Yori Akai (Blood Is Redder Than The Sun)**, **Hikisareta Joji (Torn Lust)**, and **Shiro No Jinzo Bijo (White Baby Doll)**.

9 • Wakamatsu's use and admixture of "found" music and original scoring is one of the most striking aspects of **Embryo**, and indeed his subsequent movies. Church organ, baroque hapsichord, soul-rending lullabyes and, in particular, his use of strident classical themes to counterpoint moments of sickening violence (clearly anticipating Kubrick's use of same in **A Clockwork Orange** [GB, 1971]), weave a potent sonic fabric to which he would later add avant-garde jazz and weird folk ballads (see **Shojo Geba**

Geba, for example).

10 • In the course of their investigation the police began to suspect that Richard Speck, the nurse-killer of Chicago, was also responsible for a series of still unsolved sex murders in the area of the Great Lakes. He had, after all, been there at the time of the crimes. The tattooed "rockabilly-killer" (complete with Elvis quiff and leather jacket) was duly sentenced to imprisonment for life ("600 years") without remission.

11 • Though Wakamatsu's theory that Speck spared the nurse out of sympathy [see interview] is, of course, mistaken.

Wakamatsu's **Nihon Boko Ankokushi: Ijosha No Chi (Underground History Of Japanese Sex Violence: Blood Of A Stranger,** 1967) was also based on true crime, loosely reprising – with typical embellishments of sadism and political disharmony – the story of Yoshio Kodaira, a notorious Tokyo rapist in the 1940s. Wakamatsu continued with a series of **Underground History Of Japanese Sex Violence** films, including: **Zoku Nihon Boko Ankokushi: Bogyaku Ma (Underground History Of Japanese Sex Violence 2: Rank Oppressive Evil,** 1967); **Nihon Boko Ankokushi: Onju (Underground History Of Japanese Sex Violence: Raging Beast,** 1970); and **Gendai Nihon Boko Ankokushi (Story From The Underground History Of Japanese Sexual Violence,** 1972).

Other films Wakamatsu directed in 1967 include **Sei Hanzai (Sex Crimes), Mitsu (Dark Streets), Ami No Naka No Boko (Rape Trap), Sei No Horo (Sex Beast),** and **Ranko (Orgy).**

Shuji Terayama's **Emperor Tomato Ketchup**

12 • Juro Kara is a radical figure in "post-Shingeki theatre", an avant-garde theatre movement which developed parallel to Japanese New Wave cinema in the 1960s, fomenting in the decadent Golden Gai area of Shinjuku. Kara is director of the Jokyo Gekijo ("Situation") Theatre, whose itinerant troupe, Akai Tento, have performed works such as *Hebi Hime* (*Snake Princess,* 1977) to continued acclaim. Kara co-scripted **Violated Angels,** as well as playing the lead role. He also appears (as himself) in

Oshima's **Diary Of A Shinjuku Thief**, and more recently in **Last Frankenstein** (1992), a film by modern cult theatre director Takeshi Kawamura. Kara's only film as director is **Genkai Nada (Dead Horizon**, 1976).

Other key post-Shingeki playwrights include Makoto Satoh and Shuji Terayama. Satoh is best known for his plays *Abe Sada No Inu* ("Sada Abe's Dogs") and *Onna-goroshi Abura No Jigoku* ("Woman Killer In Oil Hell"), while Terayama received acclaim for such scandalous works as *Inugami* ("Dog God", 1969) and *Jashumon* ("Gate Of Heretics", 1971), performed by his travelling Tenjo Sajiki troupe. Terayama moved into movies properly in 1970 with the short **Tomato Ketchup Kotei (Emperor Tomato Ketchup)**, a typical melange of nudity and libidinal regression concerning the sexual adventures of a nine-year-old boy. Terayama's later films include **Rolla** (1974), **Marudororu No Uta (The Songs Of Maldoror**, 1977) and the French/Japanese production **Les Fruits De La Passion (Fruits Of Passion** *aka* **Story Of O II**, 1981), starring Klaus Kinski. His absurdist credo is betrayed by the following quote: "I believe my films are very funny, whilst having the appearance of being serious; today, the greatest sickness is taking oneself seriously".

Shuji Terayama's **Fruits Of Passion**

The collision of film and the avant-garde is best represented by Katsu Kanai's **Mujin Retto (The Deserted Reef**, 1969), a grotesque and surrealistic visual poem suffused with alarmingly cruel, absurd and perverse imagery. Kanai's **Okuku (The Kingdom**, 1973) is an equally strange creation, in which a deranged bird-watcher must pass through the anus of a duck in order to defy his nemesis, King Chronos.

The spirit of post-Shingeki and its links to underground cinema still survive in today's Tokyo, maintained by the likes of Kei Fujiwara, star of **Tetsuo** and director of **Organ** [see chapter 8], who runs her own avant-garde playhouse.

13 • The Marquis de Sade's credo of sexual violence, blasphemy, revolution, cosmic atavism and the annihilation of the nuclear family is encapsulated in his *Philosophy In The Boudoir* (1798), a polymorphous rite which ends with the mother – the eternal betrayer – being punished by having her vagina sewn shut (also symbolically denying re-entry to the sundered foetus). Sade took these codes to their murderous conclusion in *The 120 Days Of Sodom*, in which his libertines devise endless ways to fornicate with and then butcher mothers, daughters, prostitutes, pregnant women and little girls alike. The Sadean impulses which drive Wakamatsu's **The Embryo Hunts In Secret** reach fruition in **Violated Angels**, an absolute indictment of the human condition expressed with perverse, poetic savagery.

Tatsumi Kumashiro's **Onna Jigoku: Mori Wa Nureta (Female Hell: Wet Forest,** 1973) is a notable *roman porno* film partially based on de Sade's *Juliette*.

14 • **Haragashi Onna (Womb To Let), Kikutai No Yokkyu (Desires Of The Flesh), Fukushu Ki (Demon Of Vengeance)**, and **Kimpeibai (Concubines)**.

*Koji Wakamatsu's **Death Of A Madman***

15 • Other films directed by Wakamatsu in 1969 include **Kyoso Joshiko (Death Of A Madman), Niku No Hyoteki Tobo (Screaming Flesh Target), Kongai Joji (Adulterous Lust), Gendai Sei Hanzai Zekkyohen: Ryu Naki Boko (Modern Sex Crimes: Fierce Screams, Wild Rape), Gendai Sei Hanzai Ankokuhen: Aru Torima No Kokuhaku (Modern Sex Crimes: Confessions Of A Demon Killer)**, and **Otoko Goroshi Onna Goroshi: Hadaka No Judan (Male Killer, Female Killer, Naked Bullet)**.

16 • In a legendary aside to his collaborator Atsushi Yamatoya – a notorious agoraphobic – as they surveyed the panorama of the film's events, Wakamatsu urged Yamatoya to "lock yourself inside here".

17 • Pier Paolo Pasolini's **Salo: O Le 120 Giornati Di Sodoma** (Italy, 1975) is his version of the Marquis de Sade's atrocity bible *The 120 Days Of Sodom*. Pasolini transposes the book's action to an Italian castle at the end of World War II, producing an annihilating meditation on fascism and absolute corruption. **Salo** remains the most faithful cinematic interpretation of de Sade.

*Koji Wakamatsu's **The Angelic Orgasm***

18 • The Angelic Orgasm was actually withdrawn by its distributors – fearful of "copycat" crimes – when a spate of real-life terrorist bombings occurred. Around this time, Wakamatsu himself reportedly left Japan to "join" the Palestinian Liberation Front. In 1971 he and Masao Adachi produced the short film **Sekigun PFLP: Sekai Senso Sengen (Red Army PFLP: World War Statement)** in Palestine. His name has also been (tenuously) linked to similar organizations within Japan, such as the Red Army who in 1971 executed twelve of their own rank in a public purge known as The Summation.

SADOMANIA

THE JOYS OF TORTURE

"Torture was used invariably and routinely for exacting confessions throughout Japanese history. With such precedents, the association in the popular imagination has spawned patterns of sado-masochism quite different from Europe and the United States."

—Oniroku Dan, novelist

"(S/M) is different in Japan. It is not about mutual enjoyment. This has to be seen against the relevant position of Japanese women in society. In Japan the world of S/M is often connected with military uniforms... S/M power and authority are presented as paranoiac themes. S/M exposes the cruelty of absolute power by showing this in a violent way to the viewer."

—Masami Akita, musician/filmmaker

SADOMASOCHISTIC themes of bondage, torture, and rape against women figure prominently in pink cinema, nor is there any taboo against these acts – viewed as aberrant in Western society – to prevent them featuring in mainstream Japanese culture. As far back as the likes of Seijun Suzuki's **Gate Of Flesh**, in the years when pink film was yet to become fully established, scenes of female bondage and rope torture appeared in dramas of varying kinds.[1] In the mid-1960s Koji Wakamatsu introduced such themes into his underground films with unflinching depictions of cruelty and wanton violence, yet these independent productions were generally marginalised due to their "experimental" or perceived political nature. But slowly more mainstream productions from the bigger studios, such as Akira Inoue's

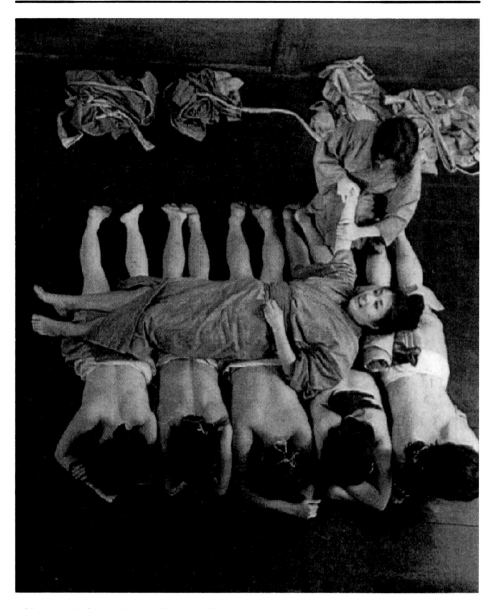

*Akira Inoue's **Secret Report From A Women's Prison***

Hiroku Onna-ro (Secret Report From A Women's Prison, Daiei Studios, 1967) and Baku Komori's **History Of Torture And Punishment** (Dokuritsu Studios, 1967) started to appear, in which the torture of women was less an adjunct to the plot than the actual *raison d'être* of the film. This was exemplified by the Toei Studios production **Tokugawa Onna Keibatsu Shi (Criminal Women**, 1968). Directed by Teruo Ishii in Kyoto, **Criminal Women** proved to be merely the first in a series of some eight films made between 1968 and 1973, which became known collectively as the **Joys Of Torture** series. With the exceptional of one male-oriented entry – **Yakuza Keibatsu Shi: Rinchi! (Yakuza Torture History: Lynching!**, 1969) – the films

Teruo Ishii's **Orgies Of Edo**

are basically about the incarceration, whipping, binding, stretching, and general torturing of women, from historical times to present-day. These films clearly belong to the genre of Japanese exploitation movies known as *ero-guro* – short for "erotic-grotesque".[2]

Ishii was an accomplished film-maker,[3] and **Criminal Women** is technically more proficient than many subsequent films in the genre, despite its clinical approach to its subject matter – sadism. Ishii's films are at least redeemed by a plot, providing actual motivation for the punishments which are inevitably inflicted upon the female characters. **Criminal Women**, like the majority of the other films in the series, is comprised of three stories. All are set in the Tokugawa period[4], and commence after a "prologue" showing three women being arbitrarily executed by decapitation, immolation and dismemberment. In the first story, a woman is arrested on suspicion of incest with her mentally-retarded brother, brutally interrogated, and finally crucified; in the second, a monk is forced to watch the lengthy torture of the nun he loves, with much emphasis placed on defiling her vagina; the third story concerns a sadist who keenly demonstrates to a tattoo artist the true expression of agony on a tortured woman's face.

The other films in the series include: **Tokugawa Onna Keizu (Tokugawa Women Bloodline, 1968)**; **Tokugawa Irezumi Shi Seme Jigoku (Tokugawa Tattoo History: Torture Hell, 1969)**; **Genroku Onna Keizu: Zankoku, Ijo, Gyakui Monogatori (Orgies Of Edo, 1969)**; **Ijo Seiai Kiroku Harenchi (Shameless: Abnormal And Abusive Love, 1969)**; **Meiji, Taisho, Showa: Ryoki Onna Hanzai Shi (Meiji, Taisho And Showa Era: Grotesque Cruelty To Women, 1969)**; and **Porno Jidai-Geki: Bohachi Bushido (Porno Samurai Theatre: Bohachi Code Of Honour, 1973)**.[5]

Other notable *ero-guro* productions with a women-in-prison theme have included the **Joshu Sasori (Scorpion: Female Prisoner, 1972/3)** series; **Hiroku Nagasaki Onna-ro (Secret Report From Nagasaki Women's Prison, Akikazu Ohta, 1976)**; the **Jitsuroku Onna Kanbetsusho (True Story Of A Woman Condemned)** trilogy (Koyu Ohara, 1975/6); **Zangyaku No Onna Gomon (Cruelty Of The Female Inquisition, Shinya Yamamoto, 1991)**; and **Onna Hanka-cho: Edo Gomon Keibatsu (Criminal Women Report: Edo Inquisition Torture, Masaru Tsushima, 1995)**. And in 1992, Shintoho Studios launched a new line of *ero-guro*, to be known as *Hard Porno*. For one of their first productions, **Gomon Hyaku-nen-shi (Torture Chronicles: 100 Years)**, they hired the legendary Koji Wakamatsu to direct. Wakamatsu duly delivered a viciously extreme but well-crafted film, featuring captive girls being whipped, crucified, raped, battered and electrocuted. He quickly followed up with **Jokei Gokinsei Hyaku-nen (Torture Chronicles Continues)**, adding necrophilia and tattoo torture to the range of graphic atrocities.

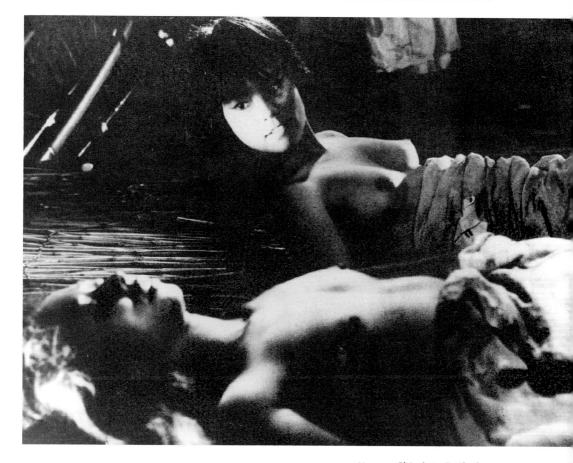

Kaneto Shindo's **Onibaba**

With the success of films like Ishii's, the strands of graphic violence evidenced in *chambara*[6] movies such as Akira Kurosawa's **Yojimbo (Bodyguard, 1962)**[7] or Masaki Kobayashi's **Seppuku (Ritual Suicide, 1962)**, had clearly combined with the often misogynistic sexual motifs of the emergent pink format to form a virulent new sub-genre, which would quickly establish itself in the Japanese marketplace.

The bad seeds of this collision of sex and violence can be traced back to films like Morihei Magatani's **Kyuju-Kyuhonme No Kimusume (Blood Sword Of The 99th Virgin, 1959)**, but the demon flower first blossoms with Kaneto Shindo's **Onibaba** (*aka* **The Hole** *aka* **Devil Woman, 1964)**[8], a devastating "horror" movie motivated by erotic compulsion and sexual jealousy. In feudal Japan, a middle-aged woman and her daughter-in-law are marsh-dwellers, scavenging from dead *samurai* to make ends meet. They sleep topless. Fearing her husband killed at war, the girl commences an affair with his comrade Hachi, who now lives nearby. Their crazed lust is evoked in beautiful moonlit shots, soundtracked by thunderous drums, as they rush through the tall reeds to meet and consummate their passion. In the midst of this psychogeographical nightscape lies the hole itself, a repository for the looted corpses, resembling a monstrous vagina as we view it from above.

Jealousy and fear of abandonment spur the elder woman to desperate

Kaneto Shindo's **Onibaba**

measures. She kills a passing *samurai* and tears off his demonic warmask, revealing a hideously disfigured face beneath. She wears the mask by night, scaring the girl away from her trysts with Hachi, until finally it becomes stuck fast to her face. In a harrowing scene of primal violence, her daughter-in-law smashes on the mask with a hammer, relishing every blow, until it finally splits away to reveal the mother-in-law's face as badly scarred as the *samurai's*. By oppressing sexuality, she has become as one with those who oppressed her, the hated *samurai*, and her only recourse is to plunge headfirst into the hole itself in a frenzied climax of pandemoniac proportion.

This blend of sex and horror was taken up by exploitation studios like Koei, and productions such as **Bed Of Violent Desires, Ten Years Of Evil, Vicious Doctor, Virgin Cruelty**, or Nikkatsu's **White Skin In The Dark**; films featuring disfigured or mutilated women, erotic mania, gruesome sex murders and bloody retribution. And once the all-pervasive Nikkatsu had introduced S/M into their pink movies, there could be no turning back. Violent sex proved equally as popular as torture/punishment. Amongst the crudest perpetrators in this newly-legitimised arena was the director Giichi Nishihara, whose ultra-sleazy excursions include **Grotesque Perverted Slaughter** (1976), **Abnormal Passion Case: Razor** (1977), and **I'll Rape You Whenever I Want** (1977). These works fall firmly into the

Nikkatsu's **White Skin In The Dark**

category of *ero-guro*, with more emphasis on actual sex punctuated by moments of extreme gore (such as a double leg amputation by cleaver) and, as the titles suggest, are purely concerned with abuse of women. Also working in this area, but with more sophistication, were Yu Productions, a company comprised of three filmmakers – Genji Makamura, Ryuichi Hiroki and Hitoshi Ishikawa – who collectively authored their films as "Go Ijuin". These works include **Za SM (S/M,** 1984), **Za Sekkan (Sexual Abuse,** 1985) and, most notably, **Kankin Sei No Dorei: Ikenie 2 (Captured For Sex 2,** 1987).

    Captured For Sex 2 is a full-on exposition of typical misogynistic mayhem, with minimal plot and dialogue and almost continuous sex action. A young couple's car breaks down and they are helped by a local man, who invites them back to his house. He turns out to be a vicious sadist, who captures and ties up his guests naked at knifepoint before sexually molesting the girl, Miki. First she is forced to fellate her boyfriend, Shingo, then the Sadist rapes her from behind as Shingo watches impassively. Next Shingo has to fuck Miki with a cucumber held in his teeth, while the Sadist plants a thick, lighted candle in her mouth. He ties bells tightly to her nipples then lights another two candles and pours molten wax all over her belly and breasts. He forces Shingo to drink some potent wine – "made from a snake" – and the young man finds himself becoming strangely aroused by the ongoing torture and humiliation of his girlfriend. As evening falls she tries to escape, but the Sadist catches her, shaves off her pubic hair and forces

Go Ijuin's **Captured For Sex 2**

Shingo to eat the newly-depilated pussy. After this act, which also arouses him, Shingo realises that this is the life for him; he begs to become the Sadist's apprentice, and is accepted.

The next day the two men administer Miki then leave her with a cork firmly plugged into her rectum. They drive around and eventually are able to kidnap another girl, Michiko, who they bring back to the house for more sessions of no-holds-barred, systematic abuse and torture. First – after the Sadist instructs Shingo in the use of various gynaecological and genital-torture devices – Michiko is stripped naked, bound by ropes and suspended from the ceiling; then shown in a realistic, matter-of-fact style, she is subjected to whipping, piercing by needles, and burning by a lighter. While she hangs there the plug is finally removed from the agonized Miki's anus, and pints of liquid excrement gush forth. After glass beads and spirits are funnelled into Michiko's vulva, the tone of the films lightens somewhat to allow for some prolonged lesbian action between the two girls, which then leads to enforced fellatio on both men.

Next day Miki is forced to phone one of her friends and invite her to the house for a "party". The hapless friend becomes Shingo's first solo victim; she is stripped naked, chained, whipped, ball-gagged and forced to crawl on all fours like a dog, her breasts are clamped with sharp metal clips and she is covered in hot wax. She is then raped by the Sadist, then subjected to more extreme wax torture and viciously flagellated. All three girls are then strung up high, upside-down, in a great rope rigging, while their two captors brandish blazing torches beneath them and whip them demonically.

Next day, as the girls feed from bowls like animals, Shingo abruptly stabs

*Ryuichi Hiroki's **Muma***

and murders his mentor. We next see the girls untied and dressed as the Sadist is buried in the garden, their ordeal seemingly at an end. But the film then cuts back to them naked and chained once again; Shingo, unable to return to "normal" life, has become the new master of sadism – "Nobody can ever leave this house of pleasure".

In 1992 the three filmmakers comprising Go Ijuin went their separate ways, producing such sex and violence classics as **Satsujin Ga Ippai (Orgy Of Killing,** Genji Nakamura, 1992), **Chi To Ekusutasi (Blood And Ecstasy,** Hitoshi Ishikawa, 1995) and **Muma (Dream Devil,** Ryuichi Hiroki, 1995)[9].

Countless other titles – mostly even more extreme, hardcore and cheaply-made – are available in the S/M field, with self-explanatory titles such as **Air Hostess Captured By Sex-Sadist, Because She Disobeyed, Bondage M: Skin Feast, Bound For Pleasure, Brutality Of Tortured Women, Close-Up Torture, Flesh Meat Doll, Leather Straps And Yuki, Memoirs Of A Captured Girl, Nubile Sex Slaves, Rope Hunt, Rubber Lady, Sadistic Violence To Ten Virgins, Seven Days Of Torture, Sex In Chains, Tattooed For Torture,** or **Three Days Of Sub-Human Treatment.** Possibly the only factor which prevents these crossing over from pornography to out-and-out "horror" movies is that they do, by and large, fall short of portraying the actual murder of women [see chapter 6].

Amidst this sea of cruelty for cruelty's sake, however, two films in particular stand out as examples of the S/M motif used to create authentic

Yasuzo Masumura's **Moju**

documents of *amour fou*. Yasuzo Masumura's **Moju (Blind Beast**, 1969)[10] and
Nagisa Oshima's **Ai No Koriida (Ai No Corrida** *aka* **Empire Of The Senses** *aka* **In
The Realm Of The Senses**, 1976 [see chapter 4]) both achieve a claustrophobic,
violent sexual delirium whose intensity remains unequalled by anything in
Western cinema.

Based on a story by Edogawa Rampo[11], **Moju** opens with an array of
erotic still images, photographs at an exhibition[12]. Aki (played by Mako Midori),
the beautiful young fashion model who posed for these elegant bondage shots,
is startled to see a blind man fondling a nude statue of her with near-religious
ecstasy. Disturbed by this sight, and by the neural responses she senses in her own
body, she quits the gallery. That evening she books a masseur, and a blind man[13]
in white coat and white stick duly turns up at her flat. She soon becomes annoyed
when the man's caresses begin to take on a sexual nature, following the contours
of her breasts and buttocks. She orders him to leave, but he suddenly grabs her
and chloroforms her. As she struggles she dislodges his dark glasses and recognises
him from the gallery. At that point the man's mother, who has been waiting
outside, enters the apartment and they smuggle the unconscious girl away to
their isolated house in the country.

Aki awakens to find herself imprisoned in a tenebrous, nightmarishly
claustrophobic environment. It seems that the man, Michio (played by Eiji

Yasuzo Masumura's **Moju**

Funakoshi), is himself a sculptor, and she is trapped in the strange domain he has moulded for himself within the walls of the old house. Through the gloom of this lightless sanctum she slowly sees that the walls are adorned with sculptures of human body parts; three-dimensional montages of huge (cataracted) eyes, noses, mouths, legs, anuses, arms, ears, and breasts cover every surface in surrealistic, Daliesque anatomical blocks. In the middle of Michio's octagonal lair lie two enormous, 60-foot sculptures of the female body, one lying face up, one face down. Most of the film's action and dialogue takes place on the lunar surface of these sexual monoliths, Aki perched between two huge breasts while Michio speaks to her, idly fondling a gigantic nipple, beneath the gaze of a labyrinth of eyes. It is in this isolated, feverishly fetishistic zone that the film's tale of fatal obsession unfurls.

Michio declares to Aki his intent to sculpt a statue of her. She attempts escape but is again captured and chloroformed, slumped between a pair of giant buttocks. The sculpting commences. Aki poses resentfully, submitting to his groping. After dinner she feigns food poisoning, and as Michio searches for medicine she tries to sneak out of the house. This time Michio's mother catches her, and she is once more shoved back into the dark chamber.

The sculpture continues. As the days pass, Aki tries a new ploy, playing up to Michio's advances, enjoining him in sexual play and allowing him to caress her

naked breasts. Michio's mother becomes jealous, and tension mounts as the sculpture slowly begins to take shape. One night, the mother can bear it no longer and helps Aki to escape. Yet again, Michio intervenes. A three-way struggle ensues with Aki blaming the mother, who finally leaps on Aki and tries to strangle her. Michio, pulling her off, crashes her into a table and kills her. As he grieves, Aki makes a last attempt at escape, but inevitably the door is locked tight and Michio eventually bundles her back to his lair.

With the death of Michio's mother comes rapid degeneration. Winter

comes and the pair remain locked in the dungeon. With the statue complete, they are now seen exploring each other's naked bodies relentlessly, still couched on the huge sculptures. Aki, herself now blinded by months of darkness, is reconciled to Michio's tactile world. She becomes enslaved by his ideals, a willing canvas for his erotic designs. Their "love-making" descends rapidly to a sado-masochistic level – a living paradigm of Georges Bataille's assertion that "sexual union is fundamentally a compromise, a half-way house between life and death". They bite each other, tearing away strips of skin; Aki is next seen heavily bound by ropes while Michio whips her mercilessly. The sexual delirium (denoted by undulating shots of the wall sculptures) intensifies; Michio drives a chisel into Aki's thigh (with a particularly unpleasant sound-effect) and sucks blood from the open wound; she reciprocates. Finally – bloody, wasted, and half-dead – they reach the ultimate conclusion of their psychosexual death trip. Aki consents to become the "perfect statue"; Michio fetches a meat cleaver and hammer, and one by one amputates her limbs with hideous blows.[14] As she dies, her pose perfectly mirroring that of the statue, Michio turns the blade on his own stomach and commits ritualistic suicide, disembowelling himself. His body falls onto hers, two blind maimed corpses forever entombed in a mausoleum of grotesque fetishes. Fade out.

In **Moju**, director Masumura has produced an outrageous masterpiece, piling Oedipal mania and primal fear onto an already malignant collage of obscenely voyeuristic and fetishistic motifs. The final descent into sexual insanity and mutual destruction evinces a unique monomaniacal intensity, compounded by the oneiric set designs and the compelling performances of the two main actors. Beautifully photographed and offset by a hauntingly baroque score, **Moju** remains a sublime cinematic achievement.

Of all the dominant themes in Japanese *ero-guro*, two in particular – bondage/rope torture and, especially, rape – undoubtedly appear the most aberrant to Western sensibilities. *Kinbaku* (rope bondage) is actually an ancient Japanese art form, and is currently upheld in its purest form by the Kinbiken organization. Kinbiken, who claim to possess the only complete archive of the history of sado-masochism in Japan, have produced dozens of rope bondage videos over the last decade. The organization is presided over by the "rope-master" Chimuo Nureki, who has the reputation in Japan of being the *sensei* ("absolute master") of his art. Nureki himself believes he was predestined to the

Mr Nureki and Masami Akita (camera) making a kinbaku video (© Romain Slocombe)

art of *kinbaku*: "According to my mother, my first act after being born was to grasp a piece of string". As well as mastering traditional rope forms, Nureki invents many of his own and names each individually. He claims to have tied up over 3,000 models.

Though the models in Kinbiken videos are usually topless, there is no sex *per se*; there is seldom any plot or dialogue, rather each video is a stark document featuring a model in a certain setting and situation, and the artistry of her binding (whether by rope, rubber tubing, plastic tape or even bandages) is as much the focus as the sexual/torture aspect. Genitals are never shown, not even fogged, although the hand-held camera often picks up a white-pantied crotch or rear. Extreme close-ups of body areas like the face are also common. The girls are generally suspended from the ceiling, but may just as easily appear bound in wheelchairs, on a beach, on a dungeon floor or shoved into a closet. Once bound, they may be subject to further humiliation or punishment such as caning, whipping, prodding, nose-hooks, being scrubbed down with a hard brush, and – most especially – nipple-torture. The latter ranges from the application of clamps and pegs to being roughly milked. Among the best-known Kinbiken models are Yuri Sunohara (also a manager of the organization), Hiromi Saotome, Yuko

Yasuharu Hasebe's **Rape!!**

Noguchi, Naomi Sugishita and, perhaps most famous of all, the buxom Kyoko Nakamura. Their films have basic titles (**Naomi Sugishita In Bondage, Kyoko Nakamura In Bondage**, etc), though some are more descriptive, e.g. **Mad Masturbator In A Gasmask**. Despite their seemingly bizarre nature, Kinbiken videos are regarded as specialist, as opposed to porn/underground, productions.

The Japanese attitude to rape, as seen both in pink productions and other film genres, is perhaps the hardest for Western viewers to entertain. It is not just the frequency with which violent rape of women occurs in these films, but in particular its apparent condoning, which confuses/offends. Generally speaking, the women in pink films fall in love with their rapists, and end up begging for more[15]; the victims are stereotypical innocents such as schoolgirls, nurses and nuns, young brides etc. A good example is Yasuharu Hasebe's **Okasu!!** (Rape!!, 1976). In this mass-market Nikkatsu production, a timid, virgin librarian is attacked and viciously raped in an elevator. Far from being traumatised by this violent assault, she finds herself enlightened to the wonders of sex and starts to sleep with as many men as she can pick up. She soon discovers that she is unable to achieve orgasm outside the savage, violatory realm of rape, and tracks down the man who originally raped her and ignited the spark of sexual lust in her. He is now the only man who can satisfy her. **Rape!!** stars Naomi Tani, probably the greatest S/M *roman porno* actress of them all[16].

映倫 ヤ

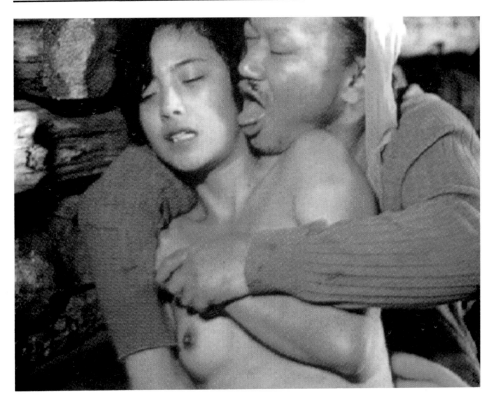

Takashi Ishii's **Angel Guts: Red Porno**

In Norifumi Suzuki's **Dabide No Hoshi: Bishoujo-gari (Star Of David: Beauty Hunting**, 1979), the protagonist is conceived when a housebreaker rapes a woman in front of her husband. The boy, Tatsuya, grows up with the same tendencies as his violent, perverted progenitor, even converting the basement of his house into a torture chamber for the abuse of women. Tatsuya is finally reunited with his father, and they team up to inflict further atrocities on helpless girls. Based on a *manga*[17] strip by Masaki Soto (of which an animated film series was also made), the film's theme exemplifies the strong Japanese belief in inherited traits as well as an apparent tolerance of rape.

The rape theme occurs again and again in pink film, from Giichi Nishihara's **Mo Ichido Yatte (Please Rape Me Again**, 1976) to Koji Wakamatsu's **Mizu No Nai Pool (Pool Without Water**, 1982) to Shinsuke Inoue's **Kankin Tobo: Utsukushiki Emonotachi (Raped In Heaven: Beautiful Humiliation**, 1995); yet it can also feature in more "mainstream" movies, from the *samurai* series **Hanzo The Blade** [see note 6] to the animation classic **Urotsukidoji** [see note 17]. Vicious and often homicidal rapists, whose assaults are shown in lingering, graphic detail, feature in psycho crime films like **Zero Onna (Zero Woman**, 1993), **Samayoeru Nozui (Roaming Tortured Brain**, 1993) and **Toriko (Victim**, 1995) – to the extent that the plot seems merely a device to pass time between violations. The whole **Tenshi No Harawata (Angel Guts)** series, which commenced in 1978, is comprised of tenebrous, stylishly-filmed psycho-dramas which largely revolve around rape. Based on the original *manga* strip of the same name by Takashi Ishii, the most striking films include **Tenshi No Harawata: Akai Inga (Angel Guts: Red Porno**,

Hisayasu Sato's **Rape Of Office Ladies**

1981), **Tenshi No Harawata: Akai Memai (Angel Guts: Red Dizziness, 1988), and Tenshi No Harawata: Akai Senko (Angel Guts: Red Lightning, 1994). Angel Guts: Red Porno,** for instance, the story of a store employee who poses for bondage pictures and is found out, consists largely of scenes of rape, voyeurism and feverish masturbation (including the use of a condom-covered table-leg as an oversized dildo). Particularly unpleasant is a sequence in which a stocking-masked rapist brutally smashes a girl unconscious, strips and violates her, then urinates over her nude breasts and leaves her in a pool of blood. Ishii himself scripted the films, and also directed several of them[18].

Rape remains a popular theme in the "New Wave" porn cinema of Hisayasu Sato and his peers [see chapter 5]. Sato himself has weighed in with such gems as **OL Boko Kegasu (Rape Of Office Ladies, 1986), Shimai Renzoku Rape: Eguru! (Serial Rape Of Sisters: Gouge It Out!, 1989), Tejobokoma Itaburu! (Maniac Rapist With Handcuffs: Torment!, 1990), OL Renzoku Rape: Kyonyu Musaboru (Serial Rape Of Office Ladies: Devour Big Tits, 1990), Renzoku Rape: Hentaijikken (Serial Rape: Perversion Experiments, 1990),** and **Lesbian Rape: Amai Mitsuju (Lesbian Rape: Sweet Syrup, 1991).**

But maybe most outrageous of all is the notorious **Reipuman (Rapeman)** series, which commenced in 1990 and again derives from *manga*. The first six episodes are directed by Takao Nagaishi, and star Hiroyuki Okita as Rapeman. "Classic" rapist iconography – handcuffs, ski-masks etc – decorates the video sleeves of these alarming films. The premise is simple: Rapeman Services (motto: "righting wrongs through penetration") exists to bring unruly or misbehaved women into line. Male clients gladly enlist the help of Rapeman to punish unfaithful wives, cheating girlfriends etc, by brutally raping them. Although this concept is alien to Western ways of thinking[19], the **Rapeman** series is massively

Hisayasu Sato's **Maniac Rapist With Handcuffs: Torment!**

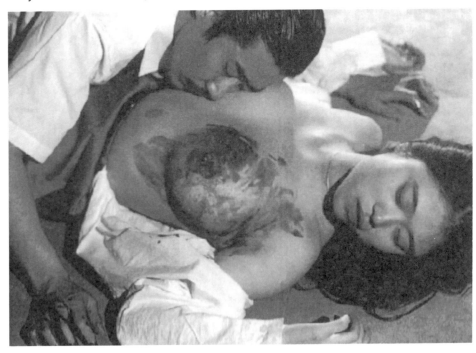

Hisayasu Sato's **Serial Rape Of Office Ladies: Devour Big Tits**

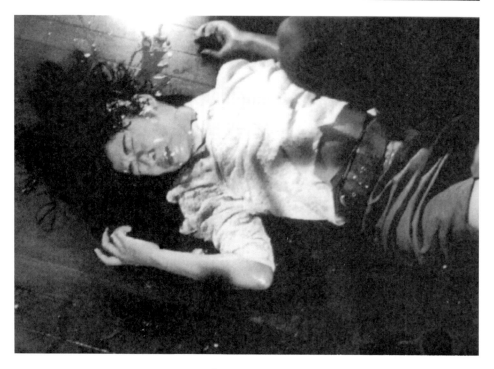

*Hisayasu Sato's **Serial Rape: Perversion Experiments***

popular, mainstream entertainment in Japan;[20] the film's relatively light-hearted tone will either alleviate, or add to, its shock value, depending on your particular viewpoint.

1 • Glimpses of straightforward screen nudity were not uncommon even in the 1950s, as in Suzuki's own **Rajo To Kenju (Nude Girl With A Gun, 1957)**. The trend was sneakily initiated by Shintoho Studios in the mid-'50s with a new genre, the "girl diver" movie. Girls were shown wet-bloused, then later topless, then later even naked as they dived for pearls in such films as **Onna Shinjuo No Fukushu (Revenge Of The Pearl Queen)** and **Ama No Bakemono Yashiki (Haunted House Of Ama** aka **Girl Divers Of Spook**

Mansion). Nudity soon occurred in other genre films – for instance Koji Seki's **Joyoku No Tanima (Valley Of Carnal Desires,** 1963) which featured daring footage of a naked "jungle woman" – paving the way for pink cinema proper. More recent entries in the persistent "girl diver" sub-genre include Atsushi Fujiura's **Yobai Ama (Nasty Diver,** 1977) and **Shikijo Ama (Lusty Diver,** 1981).

2 • This term in fact dates back to the pre-War period. In Japanese populist art and literature, the '20s and '30s were known as the era of *eroguronansensu* – "erotic/ grotesque nonsense" – as epitomised by magazines such as Umehara Hokumen's *Hentaishiryo,* silk-screen artist Ito Seiu, and the writer Edogawa Rampo [see also note 11].

3 • Ishii made various adventure and gangster movies for Toei, as well as the notable, grotesque horror entry **Kyofu Kikei Ningen (Horror Of A Deformed Man,** 1969). His 1970 horror production **Kaidan Nobori Ryu (Blind Woman's Curse)** was made for Nikkatsu and includes a fair amount of sadism, for example a demented hunchback who skins women alive. Of the **Joys Of Torture** movies, Ishii told Romain Slocombe in a 1998 interview: "The idea came from the head of the company. I did some research on documents from the period. That world was quite unknown, I thought that filming this would make me come up with some interesting ideas. I had no preconceived ideas when I started. We researched tortures and punishments of the Edo period, but didn't use everything we discovered. There were some things worse than what appeared in our films!"

4 • Also known as the Edo period (Edo being the former name for Tokyo), the Tokugawa period lasted from approximately 1616 to 1868, during which time some fifteen generations of Tokugawa Shogun (military overlords) ruled Japan under a feudal system. Society was divided into different classes, headed by the *samurai* –

sword-bearing aristocrats skilled in military and martial arts, but also highly educated in philosophy. Their code of honour, *bushido*, demanded the utmost fidelity and virtue, and to abuse it was a disgrace that demanded atonement in the extreme form of *seppuku* – ritual suicide by disembowelling before being decapitated. Most *samurai* were attached to the lord of a dominion. These lords comprised the land-owning class, or the Daimyo. Dispossessed, wandering *samurai* were known as *ronin*. Nearly all the rest of the Japanese population were peasants, whose lot in life was to serve the Daimyo and the Shogun, and lowlier even than them was a common class of outcasts comprised of beggars, prostitutes, freaks, lepers and the like.

Much treachery involving the Shogunate and the Daimyo was perpetrated in the Tokugawa period, often involving *ronin* and the stealthy spies and assassins known as *ninja*. While these martial activities form the basis for most films set in the Tokugawa period [see note 6], pink movie-makers have also utilised this feudal *mise-en-scène* on many occasions. Apart from Ishii's salacious tracts on female punishment, scenarios involving the Shogun's harem of concubines have provided ample opportunity for exploiting groups of naked women, with plentiful lesbian action thrown in. Films in this vein include Isao Hayashi's **Irogoyami: Ohuku Hiwa (Eros Schedule Book: Concubine Secrets** *aka* **Castle Orgies**, 1971); Norifumi Suzuki's **Shikijo Daimyo (The Sex-Crazed Daimyo**, 1971); and Ikuo Sekimoto's **Ooku Ukiyo-buro (Concubine Palace**, 1976).

5 • Toei continued the theme with the likes of Yuji Makiguchi's **Joy Of Torture 2**, a film of relentless, savage cruelty in which atrocities are meted out to both male and female victims in equal measure. The film comprises two Tokugawa period tales, the first about Christian persecution, the second concerning life in and around a seedy brothel. **Joy Of Torture 2** is an unapologetic catalogue of bloody violence, and even the occasional sex scenes are nearly all non-consensual. Amongst the tortures depicted are: women boiled alive, crucified, run through with spears or knives, mutilated, branded, or whipped; one woman has her legs ripped off by oxen driven in opposing directions, with resultant evisceration; a pregnant prostitute has the foetus torn from her womb by an old crone with her fist up the girl's vagina. Men are burned, cooked, hung and quartered, mutilated, crucified, run through, or castrated; one has his foot pulped by hammers and the exposed bones snapped off by hand, another is placed in the stocks and has his neck sawn through by a retard with a serrated machete. Again, this is not some clandestine gore video, but a quality feature film produced by one of the biggest studios in Japan.

6 • *Chambara* ("swordfight") movies, usually set in the Tokugawa period and featuring the exploits of feudal *samurai* and *ronin*, have always been the popular mainstay of *jidai-geki* (historical films, usually produced in Kyoto). Although the popularity of these movies faded in the 1920s and 1930s with the advent of *gendai-geki* (modern-style films) and *shomin-geki* (films about the middle classes), *chambara* underwent a renaissance in the post-war Japan of the 1950s, with prestigious directors such as Akira Kurosawa and Masaki Kobayashi seeing an opportunity to make statements on contemporary Japan through period drama. With popular actor Toshiro Mifune as his regular male lead, Kurosawa brought dirty realism to the *chambara* genre evoking a world of immorality, violence and sudden death; in **Yojimbo**, for instance, the brutal tone is set early on with the appeareance in the street of a mongrel with a severed human hand in its jaws. (**Yojimbo** was remade, with some style, by Italian director Sergio Leone as **A Fistful Of Dollars**, with Clint Eastwood in the Mifune role; Kurosawa was less lucky with his classic **Seven Samurai**, which was desecrated as the moronic Hollywood western **Magnificent Seven**.) Other directors to gain renown for *chambara* movies include Hideo Gosha, Kihachi Okamoto and Kinji

Akira Kurosawa's **Yojimbo**

Fukasaku (with **Conspiracy Of The Yagyu Clan**, 1978). More recent genre entries of note are scant, but include Mitsumasa Sato's **Black Magic Wars** (1983) and Kaizo Hayashi's phantasmic **Zipang** (1991).

Chambara films flourished into the 1960s and peaked in the early '70s, with the violence (and occasional sex) growing increasingly fast, bloody and explicit in such popular series as **Zatoichi (Blind Swordsman**, 1962–72); **Kyoshiro Nemuri (Son Of Black Mass** *aka* **Sleepy Eyes Of Death**, 1963–69); **Gokuaku Bozu (Wicked Priest**, 1968–70); **Goyokiba (Hanzo The Blade** *aka* **Razor Hanzo**, 1972–74); **Shurayukihime (Lady Snowblood**, 1973–74); and, best of all, **Kozure Ookami (Lone Wolf With Cub** *aka* **Baby Cart**, 1972–74). Based on the epic *manga* by Kazuo Koike and Goseke Kojima (who also created *Lady Snowblood* and *Hanzo The Blade*, amongst many others), the **Lone Wolf** series commenced with Kenji Misumi's **Kozure Ookami: Ko O Kashi Ude Kashi Tsukamatsuru (Lend A Child, Lend An Arm**, 1972), in which we are introduced to the character of Itto Ogami (played by Tomisaburo Wakayama) – lethal swordsman and *kaishakunin*, official executioner to the Shogun – and his son Daigoro (played by Akihiro Tomikawa), whom he pushes around the country in a baby cart equipped with hidden weapons. Driven into exile by the Shogun, and also pursued by the evil Yagyu clan, Ogami is now an itinerent *ronin* on a career of evil, forced to perform assassinations for money. The violence is graphic and eruptive, culminating in a spectacular duel between Ogami and the son of the Yagyu chief; but Misumi's sequel, **Kozure Ookami: Sanzu No Kawa No Ubaguruma (Baby Cart At The River Styx**, 1972), is the visual masterpiece of the series.

River Styx – at times resembling the cinema of Sergio Leone with its extreme close-ups, circling camera, soundtrack of distorted whistles and chimes, and long periods of stillness punctuated by explosive violence – is virtually operatic in its depiction of bloodletting. The blood in **River Styx** is bright red, and it sprays from puncture wounds in long pulsing pressure jets that hiss like escaping air. Ogami's foe

Scene from the **Zatoichi** *series*

Kenji Misumi's **Baby Cart At The River Styx**

– male and female alike – are impaled on spears, their heads are sliced open or even sliced clean in half like melons, throats cut agape, girl *ninja* have their breasts slashed open, clansmen's feet are cut off by the whirling wheel-knives of Daigoro's baby cart.

Elsewhere, a Yagyu killer is cut to ribbons by girl *ninja*: ears, fingers, nose, legs and arms are all hacked off until he is just a faceless torso rolling on the ground in a river of blood; later three bodyguards, the Brothers of Death, kill by a nailed club smashing skulls, spiked glove gouging into faces, metal claw plunging through chests or driving into the skulls of hidden spies to drag them, screaming and fountaining blood, from their vigil beneath the desert dunes. And amidst this carnage, almost surreal in its imaginative scope and the inventiveness of its startling juxtapositions, are scenes of provocative beauty: an infant strumming a girl assassin's nipple, a burning ship spiralling into ash, a sword spinning silently, sparkling, to an ocean grave.

Kenji Misumi also directed the two other outstanding episodes of the series: **Kozure Ookami: Shi Ni Kaze Ni Mukau Ubaguruma (Flying On The Wind Of Death** *aka* **Lightning Swords Of Death**, 1972), and **Kozure Ookami: Meifu Mado (Tread Lightly On The Road To Hell**, 1973).

There is little nudity or sex in the **Lone Wolf** series, but this is not the case in the three **Hanzo The Blade** films, whose very concept revolves around an investigator (Hanzo) with an "iron" penis; he has built up his member through rigorous training, producing an instrument of steely strength which he uses to interrogate (rape) female suspects. The first episode was made by **Lone Wolf** director Kenji Misumi, but Yasuzo Masumura's **Kamisori Hanzo Jigoku-zeme (Razor Hanzo's Torture Hell**, 1973) is the pick of the trilogy, featuring not just the usual copious and inventive blood-spilling but also a plot which allows for plenty of Hanzo's particular brand of interrogation as he investigates an illegal abortion clinic being operated by corrupt nuns.

In 1990, Takemitsu Sato directed **Jigoro Koppu (Lone Wolf Cop)**, deliberately transposing the essential character of original Lone Wolf Itto Ogami to present-day Tokyo, in the form of a tough policeman authorised to execute slave-ring gangsters without question. In the manner of Kenji Misumi's earlier *chambara* films, the killings are excessively gory, with blood spurting and spraying in rivers from bullet-holes and other heinous wounds. As in Beat Takeshi's **Sono Otoko, Kyobo Ni Tsuji (Violent Cop**, 1989) and Atsushi Muroga's outrageous **Score** (1996), the protagonist ignores all rules in pursuit of his target, resulting in a savage, blood-drenched world of nightmarish slaughter. Yet perhaps the most unrelentingly nihilistic of all *yakuza* movies came some years before, in the shape of Kinji Fukasaku's **Jingi No Hakaba (Death Of Honour** *aka* **Psycho Junkie**, 1976), a portrayal of notorious real-life assassin Rikio Ishikawa. Less reliant on excessive gunplay, the film shows Ishikawa's descent into terminal psychosis, from rape and random knife attacks as a *yakuza* soldier through heroin addiction and a series of violent murders to his final, bloody prison suicide.

Kei Fujiwara's **Organ** (1996) [see chapter 8] and Takashi Miike's **Fudoh** (1996) are two recent films which have used *yakuza* lore as the peg from which to hang extraordinarily wild and bloody narratives which spiral ever more toward the avant-garde as they progress. Based on a *manga* (comic strip) by Hiroshi Tanemura, **Fudoh** is the story of Ricky Fudoh, a young student whose handsome and cultured exterior hides dark secrets. His father is a *yakuza* crimelord, who brutally killed Ricky's brother when he was a child. Ricky is now obsessed with revenge against his father, an obsession which leads to killing and carnage on a grand scale as he recruits young assassins from his own highschool to wage war against the *yakuza* bosses. From this premise director Miike constructs a twisted world of massive violence where kids and teenage strippers become brutal and inventive killing machines, firing poison darts from their vaginas, playing football with severed heads, and flooding the screen with the torrential blood of their victims.

Closely related to the more conventional *yakuza* tales are gore-splattered martial arts movies such as the **Satsujin-ken (Iron Fist** *aka* **Streetfighter)** series (directed by Shigehiro Ozawa between 1974 and 1979), three brutal episodes in which action star Sonny Chiba plays Terry Tsuguri, another modern-day equivalent to Itto Ogami,

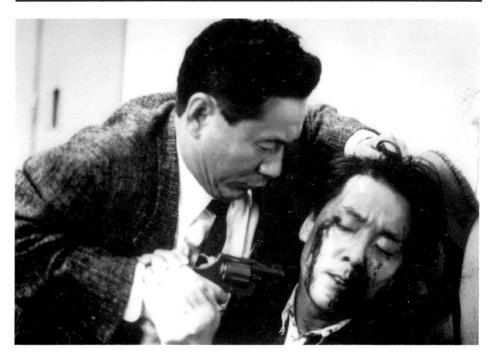

Beat Takeshi's **Violent Cop**

anti-hero of **Lone Wolf And Cub**. Tsuguri is an amoral assassin for hire who uses feet and bare hands, as opposed to *samurai* sword, to create blood-spraying carnage amongst his enemies: smashing out teeth, snapping necks, splitting skulls in half, crunching limb-bones to pulp, destroying throats, driving fingers through eye-sockets into brains, ripping off genitals, and tearing hearts still beating from shattered ribcages. Chiba also starred in the two similar **Chokugeki! Jigoku-ken (Straight Punch: Hell Fist** *aka* **Executioner)** films.

It should be noted however, that even the **Streetfighter** films seem tame and slow-paced compared to **Rikki O** (1991), a martial arts epic of near insane violence. Although based on a Japanese *manga* (comic strip), **Rikki O** is in fact a Japan/Hong Kong co-production made by a Chinese director, Lan Nai Kai; nonetheless this incredible movie deserves mention here, if only to give some perspective on levels of violence in Asian cinema as a whole. Set in a futuristic men's prison, **Rikki O** features relentless scenes of fists being driven clean through heads and bodies, limbs severed with a single blow, eyeballs smashed out, intestines used as ropes, faces cut in half by serrated machetes or sheared off by buck knives or peppered with razor blades, heads demolished, bodies smashed to pieces, crushed, blown apart and – literally – ground into hamburger meat. There is barely a moment's respite between the sequences of absurdist butchery, and **Rikki O** possibly comes the nearest yet to perfectly translating a comic strip into live-action film.

7 • Akira Kurosawa was born Tokyo, 1910. He joined Toho Studios as an assistant director in 1936, and his first film as main director was **Sugata Sanshiro** (1943). He gained Western attention with **Rashomon** (1950), and thereafter with a succession of *chambara* movies, mostly starring Toshiro Mifune. Amongst the best-known are: **Shichinin No Samurai (Seven Samurai,** 1954); **Kakushi Toride No Sanakunin (The Hidden Fortress,** 1958); and **Sanjuro** (1962).

8 • Born in Hiroshima, 1912, from farming stock, Kaneto Shindo entered the film industry in 1934, working for Shochiku. In 1950 he formed his own company, Kindai Eiga Kyokai, and went on to script many films for others as well as directing his own projects. Apart from **Onibaba**, his best-known works in the West are **Hadaka No Shima (Island, 1962)**, **Honno (Lost Sex, 1966)**, and **Yabu No Naka Kuroneko (Kureneko, 1968)**.

9 • **Dream Devil** is an elliptical Nikkatsu production which won a film award upon its release, presumably for its relatively restrained handling of themes of trauma, dream/reality, psychosis – and cigarette torture.

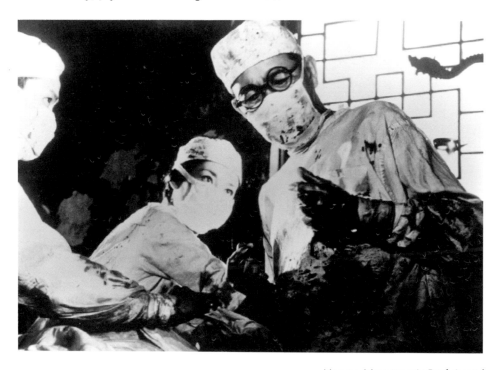

Yasuzo Masumura's **Red Angel**

10 • Born in Kofu, 1924, Yasuzo Masumura first came to Daiei Studios as an assistant director in 1948. By 1957 he was directing his own films, and his individual vision begain to shine through with **Irezumi (Spider Girl** *aka* **Tattoo, 1966)**, the lurid tale, scripted by Kaneto Shindo, of a woman branded with the black spider (a traditional mark of prostitution) and sold into slavery, who escapes to become a vicious killer of men. The same year Masumura made **Akai Tenshi (Red Angel)**. Ostensibly an anti-war statement, **Red Angel**, with its meshes of mutilation, lust, impotence, amputee sex and suicide, is very much a thematic precursor of **Moju**.

11 • Basing himself – as his adopted pen-name suggests – on Edgar Allan Poe, Rampo is the leading Japanese horror writer of the 20th century. His stories often have strong sado-masochistic elements, dealing with sex and dismemberment in equal measure. Rampo's original name is thought to be Taro Hirai. Believed born in 1894, he started writing in the 1920s, and encountered governmental censorship throughout his career due to the nature of his books. Other films to have been adapted from his stories include **Kurotokage (Black Lizard, 1962 and 1968)**; **Kyofu Kikei Ningen (Horror Of A Malformed Man, 1969)**; Noburu Tanaka's **Yaneura No Sanpo Sha (Walker In The Attic,**

Noboru Tanaka's **Walker In The Attic**

1976); **Oshie To Tabisuru Otoko (Man With The Embossed Tapestry, 1994); and Ningen Isu (Human Chair, 1997).** In 1994, director Kazuyoshi Okuyama made a centennial film version of his life, entitled simply **Rampo,** which incorporated many fantastic/surreal images in homage to the author's particular *oeuvre*.

12 • In a tribute to Charles Baudelaire, the French poet committed to derangement of the senses whose manifesto was "be drunk always", the exhibition is entitled "Fleurs Du Mai".

13 • In Japan, the blind are often trained as masseurs and their services can be booked through agencies.

14 • The dismemberment is not shown explicitly; rather, as each hammer blow falls, we see the corresponding limb drop from the statue of Aki onto the floor. What is noticeable in this climactic sequence, however, is that Aki's naked breasts – hitherto coyly concealed by clever camera angles – are now clearly displayed, as if to accentuate the sexual nature of Michio's acts of mutilation.

15 • Although this *is* the theme of Chuck Vincent's **I Want More,** an American hardcore porn film made in 1977. In the brief period in the 1970s between the acceptance of hardcore porn in the USA, and the '80s clamp-down by Ronald Reagan's Meese Commission, a number of rape-themed films such as Gerard Damiano's **Waterpower** (1975) and Helmut Richler's **Forced Entry** (1976) were in legitimate circulation in the US. Even so, unlike in Japan, these were always marginalised, taboo productions, and their acceptance was short-lived.

*Naomi Tani in Masaru Konuma's **Flower And Snake***

16 • Naomi Tani started her career with Dokuritsu Productions, a small company making pink movies with an S/M twist, such as Baku Komori's **History Of Torture And Punishment** (1967). In 1972 she directed two films for Dokuritsu, from scripts by S/M novelist Oniroku Dan: **Sex Killer** and **Hungry Sex Beast**. Her first film for Nikkatsu was **Sensual Beasts**, also in 1972. She went on to star in many S/M-themed *roman porno films*, including Masaru Konuma's **Flower And Snake**. She retired while quite young, and her last movie was **Rope And Skin**.

17 • *Manga* is the name given to modern Japanese comic books. The roots of *manga* (literally, "irresponsible pictures") stretch back centuries, to mediaeval illustrated scrolls such as *Chojugiga* ("The Animal Scrolls"), a satire by the Buddhist priest Toba, who also produced more ribald scrolls including *Yobutsu Kurabe* (*The Penis Competition*). By the 17th century, illustrated books such as *warai-bon* ("laughing books"), *makura-e* ("pillow pictures"), and *ukiyo-e* ("pictures of the floating world") were in great demand. The 19th century saw the mass production of popular woodblock picture books and prints, ranging from family stories to the violent, sadistic and bloody *muzan-e* ("atrocity prints") of artists such as Yoshitoshi Tsukioka or Yoshiiku Ochiai, and the erotic/pornographic *shunga* ("Spring pictures") of Utagawa Kuniyoshi and Shishoku Ganko. The Japanese conflation of sex and death can be seen in Utagawa Kunisada's *Peony Lantern*, a picture where one of the lovers is a skeleton.

Atrocity print by Yoshitoshi Tsukioka

Modern *manga* took shape in 20th century post-War Japan. Comic production boomed in an impoverished economy which could scarcely afford a film industry, and the influx of American culture led to the borrowing of sequential panelling and speech balloons in *manga*. The most influential *manga* artist was Osamu Tezuka, creator of strips such as *Hi No Tori* (*Firebird*), *Ribon No Kishi* (*Princess Knight*) and *Black Jack*, who introduced a cinematic technique which effectively decimated word-count and relied on codified visuals, enabling a comic to be "read" at incredible speeds. This technique has persisted, facilitating the conversion of many *manga* into actual films, whether animated or live action (eg Takashi Ishii's lurid *gekiga* ["adult graphic novel"] *Angel Guts* and, more recently, Masamune Shirow's definitive cyberpunk text *Ghost In The Shell*, filmed by Mamoru Oshii of Jigoku No Banken [Watchdogs From Hell] fame).

*Mamoru Oshii's **Ghost In The Shell***

Another writer whose *manga* have proved extremely popular when adapted to film is Go Nagai, author of scandalous '60s stories such as *Harenchi Gakuen* (*School Without Shame*), which established his trademark of highschool anarchy and sex in the classroom. Nagai's popular characters include the robot, Mazinga Z, and teen queen Cutie Honey, and his TV series have included *Battle Hawk*, *X Bomber* and *Pro Wrestling Star Aztecaizer*. His *Kekko Kamen* (*Kekko Mask*) was adapted for cinema in 1991, and the similar **Maboroshi Panti (Legendary Panty Mask)** appeared that same year. Kekko Mask is a girl superhero who patrols campus dressed only in a cape and mask, and dazzles villains with her "beautiful vagina". Panty Mask has her face concealed by a pair of leather panties as she sorts out a coven of delinquent nuns. These films are similar in concept to the **Sukeban Deka** series – schoolgirl detectives armed with razor-sharp yo-yos combat evil – which derived from the *shojo manga* ("girls' comics") of Shinji Wada, except that Nagai's are more sex-oriented. His sexy comic-strip-come-to-life world is echoed in movies like Masahiro Kasai's **Kunoichi Senshi Ninja (Female Neo-Ninjas, 1991)**, Masaru Tsushima's **Kunoichi Ninpo-cho III: Higi Densetsu No Kai (Female Ninjas: Magic Chronicles III: Sacred Book Of Sexual Positions, 1993)** – whose heroines employ such tricks as "rain of acid breast milk" and "vagina bubbles from Hell" to defeat their enemies – Hideo Tanaka's **Ojosama Deka (Girl Cop, 1994)**, and Shimako Sato's **Eko Eko Azaraku (Wizard Of Darkness, 1995)** and its sequel **Eko Eko Azaraku 2**

Shimako Sato's **Birth Of The Wizard**

(**Birth Of The Wizard**, 1996) which derive from a *manga* by Shinichi Koga.

While the majority of modern *manga* deal with everyday life, a certain percentage explicitly cover areas of extreme sex and violence. Such sado-erotic comics are known as *ero-manga*. One of the most notorious and typical examples of the genre is *Utsukushiki Kossetsu (Refracted Beauty)* by the artist Jun Hayami. Here schoolgirls are raped, tortured and eviscerated in graphic detail. Similar in tone is U-Jin's *Angel: Highschool Sexual Bad Boys And Girls Story*. In the 1970s, artist Kazuichi Hanawa produced a series of horrific, nightmarish and surrealistic works, including *Akai Yoru (Red Night)* and *Niku Yashiki (Flesh House)*. Among the major artists propagating this style are Hideshi Hino [see chapter 6] and Suehiro Maruo. Maruo's *ero-guro* depictions of murder, mutilation, sadomasochism and multiple perversions (favourite: old woman licking young boy's eyeball) hark directly back to the art of the atrocity print. Maruo is best known in the West for his *Shojo-Tsubaki (Camelia Girl*, 1984; published in English as *Mr Arashi's Amazing Freak Show*, Blast Books, New York 1991), in which the world of Tod Browning's **Freaks** (USA, 1932) is evoked and spiked with overt sexual perversion to create a universe of unrelenting horror. Director Hiroshi Harada's **Shojo-Tsubaki (Girl In The Freak Show**, 1992) is a 50-minute animated version [see chapter 8].

The full sex horrors of the most extreme *ero-manga* eventually came to the cinema screen in 1989 with **Urotsukidoji (Wandering Kid** *aka* **Legend Of The Overfiend)**, an *anime* ("animated feature") by Hideki Takayama. In this incredible psychedelic hardcore epic, the *chojin* ("overfiend") is reborn after 3,000 years. With him comes an extra-dimensional apocalypse where highschool girls are orally, vaginally and anally raped by demons with multiple twenty-foot tongues and penile tentacles, girls' faces are sprayed with phosphorescent semen before their bodies literally explode

Suehiro Maruo's Camelia Girl (© Blast Books)

*Hideki Takayama's **Wandering Kid***

in cosmic orgasms, and all manner of sexual perversion is wantonly carried out by homicidal shape-shifters hungry for "delicious pussy" after centuries in captivity. Other notable films in this explicit field of *anime* include **Adventure Kid, Blue Girl, Beauty And The Cyborgasm, Devil Man, Cream Lemon, Bondage Omen, Dreamy Express Zone,** and **Monsters On Campus.** The latter also became the basis for Kaname Kobayashi's **Inju Gakuen (Sex Beast On Campus,** 1994), a "live-action *manga*" with real actors which utilises the demonic tentacle concept of **Urotsukidoji** to salacious effect. Essentially a "pink horror" movie, **Sex Beast On Campus** shows a succession of nude and semi-nude girls being raped by a water demon whose tentacles resemble huge, sperm-drooling penises as they slide over thighs, buttocks and breasts, and in and out of wide-stretched nubile mouths. Two sequels have followed so far, and the film has also influenced the production of other trashy "tentacle" films such as Yoji Matsumoto's **Guzoo,** Mitsunori Hattori's **Inju Kyoshi (Sex Beast Teacher)** series, and the **Uratsukidoji** [sic] **(Exorsister)** movies of trash doyen Takao Nakano [see chapter 7].

Ero-manga is a flourishing genre. Recent titles of note include: *Sexcapades* by Jiro Chiba; *New Bondage Fairies* by Kondom; *Super Taboo* by Wolf Ogami; *Sexhibition* by Suehirogari; *Princess Of Darkness* by Yuichiro Tanuma; *Lust* by Tenjiku Ronin; *Countdown: Sex Bombs* by Hiroyuki Utatane; *Spunky Knight* by Kozo Yohei; *Slave To Love* by Milk Morizono; *Ogenki Clinic* by Haruka Inui; and *Misty Girl Extreme* by Toshiki Yui. Strips with these explicit, often perverse themes are deemed perfectly acceptable in Japan, where *manga* remains the single most popular medium – even Shoko Asahara's notorious Aum cult, held responsible for the 1995 nerve gas attacks in Tokyo, used *manga* to disseminate its propaganda – and comics of all kinds are read assiduously by everyone from infants to company presidents.

18.   Ishii has also directed such films as **Shinde Mo Ii (Original Sin,** 1992), **Nudo No Yoru (A Night In The Nude,** 1993), **Yoru Ga Mata Kuru (Alone In The Night,** 1994), and **Gonin (Five,** 1995). Films based on his other *manga* include Toshiharu Ikeda's **Ningyo Densetsu (Mermaid Legend,** 1984).

19.   As Steve Albini, formerly of guitar band Big Black, discovered when he called his new outfit Rapeman in honour of the series and tried to tour the UK with it. Virtually all the dates had to be abandoned due to protest, and he was forced to drop the name. It is also worth comparing the level Japanese attitude to the hysterical controversy generated in England by the showing on TV, uncut, of the crass Hollywood gang-rape drama **The Accused.**

20.   In fact, *Rapeman* is so popular that it has already been republished in well over a dozen book-format anthologies. The film version even inspired a homage, **Oshioki Haihiiru (High-Heeled Punishers,** 1994), in which a female gang are hired by abused women to take revenge on the men responsible – which they do by torturing their genitals in various ways. And, incidentally, many Japanese video stores have their own "rape" section for easy reference.

AI NO CORRIDA

IN THE REALM OF THE SENSES

"Those whom the gods would destroy they first make mad."
—Euripides

ON 16 May, 1936, an extraordinary "murder" case – in fact an astonishing crime of passion – came to light in Japan. Sada Abe, a low-class prostitute, strangled to death her lover Yoshizo (*aka* Kichizo) Ishida – believed to be a pimp – during an act of sadomasochistic love-making. This was the culmination of a sex session which apparently had lasted from 23 April to 7 May. Sada was picked up by the police as she wandered the streets in a state of strange elation. She was carrying a *furoshiki* (cloth for wrapping gifts) in which was discovered the severed penis of her dead lover. The case became notorious, and remains something of a feminist *cause célèbre* with its implications that the stereotype of submissive Japanese women is not as accurate as the patriarchal structure of their society seems to suggest.

It is this story which inspired Nagisa Oshima to make **Ai No Corrida**, a film about a fight to the death with weapons of love and passion, and a sensuality which achieves mastery over intellect.[1]

Oshima and producer Anatole Dauman had agreed to make a hardcore pornographic film, processing the print in France, where the Japanese taboo against explicit genital images did not apply. In all but the strictly mechanical sense, they failed – **Ai No Corrida** is the least pornographic film possible. The word "pornographic" devolves from the Greek *pornográphos* – "the writing of prostitutes." Inherent in this concept are connotations of loucheness and commerce. Pure sexual ecstasy and deep sexual magic have no place within it, whereas **Ai No Corrida** is an endless landscape of overwhelming emotion, sensuality and dangers which finally overtake the protagonists, who become tiny figures swamped by a giant *tsunami* ("tidal wave") created by the power of the senses.

Carnal love with all its sadness – because there is always a subtle reminder of mortality, and the acute responses of the flesh serve, paradoxically to underscore this – is the theme.

In Oshima's version of the story, Sada is a newly-employed servant at the home of Kichi, a restaurant owner. Stimulated when she spies on her new employer and his wife having sex, she soon contrives to become Kichi's mistress and the two run away together. Travelling from hotels and inns to *geisha*-houses,

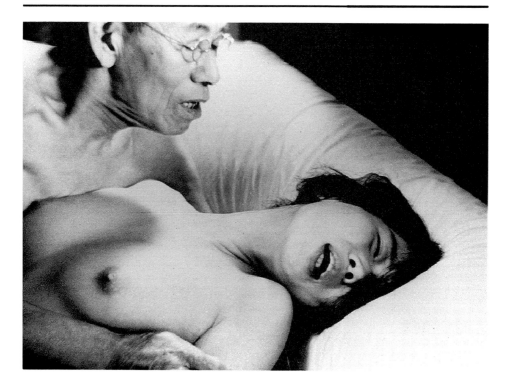

their love-making becomes obsessive and virtually non-stop, their coupling only interrupted while Sada, a former prostitute, services an elderly client; Kichi meanwhile makes love to an old *geisha* who reminds him of his mother. Sada and Kichi's erotic games quickly escalate in perversity and danger, encompassing knifeplay and asphyxiation, and leading to the film's notorious climax.

Oshima sets the mood with his titles: a screen with bars, lit from behind, where natural movements reminiscent of sea-waves or the wind playing on a gauze veil, signal a mystery which the viewer is to be allowed to penetrate. The subsidiary voyeuristic theme is thus gently introduced. The wistful softness of the image demonstrates that what will be seen is something sacred and momentous.

In some intangible subliminal way, Oshima introduces what will undoubtedly be a tragedy; much as in Shakespeare's *Othello* it is obvious from the start that there can be no happy ending. This, a kind of occult warning (as in *Othello* the concept of a great passion is always accompanied by jealousy, danger and murder) signals that what will occur is no safe flirtation.

This is maximised by Oshima's constant alternating use of night and day, light and darkness; the heroine, Sada Abe and her companion stare from an unlit hall into the brilliant sexual scene where Kichi-San, the hero, possesses his wife. Sada stakes her claim on him immediately; her face, peering through a crack in the screen, follows the undulations of his body; she enters into the act by proxy.

The swift precipitation of snow outside illustrates Sada's cold isolation, especially against the gaiety of the others as they flutter towards the market-place, where she is abruptly reminded, during an encounter with an ancient ex-client, of a past in prostitution she has deliberately forgotten. Here her character (already established as intrinsically fastidious, *viz* her rejection of a casual lesbian advance) is highlighted both by her bewilderment and the courtly way she deals with the impotent old man. However, her proprietorial attitude to the phallus is made apparent. She handles the man with a delicate assessment, and this is reprised in a later scene where she deals, far more roughly, with the penis of a small boy. (She is a respecter of weakness; virility, even in embryo, challenges her, and the masculine facet of her psyche.)

Woman empowered is an unusual concept within the Japanese social structure, and minimally illustrated when in a confrontational kitchen scene, battle is joined between Sada and the lady of the house. A verbal attack on Sada's honour brings out once more her psychic masculinity; the knife she seizes has a polyandrous usage: to defend, to attack, to castrate, and the knife as phallus.

Even when the man of the house (Kichi) enters, he is momentarily subjected to wifely criticism which he absorbs significantly without rancour. The comic/fearsome dog-mask he wears demonstrates, like the airy balloon he carries, his vulnerability – ("his bark is worse than his bite"). The knife/phallus is passed from woman to man, the control only temporarily suspended and the stage set for the *corrida* which only one will survive.

When Sada is seen on her knees, scrubbing the passage, she translates her subservience into seduction. Kichi now carries a spray of cherry-blossom. This is the *samurai* symbol of the swift passing of life – "Life is fleeting as the cherry-blossom"[2] – and the *samurai* philosophy is: "Know how to die after having known how to live."[3]

Kichi's seduction of Sada (as he sees it) is facilitated by her dubious reputation. Interestingly, the class of the *shirabyoshi*[4], the mediaeval itinerant prostitutes and female troubadours, wore a curious half-military costume which included red silk pantaloons. The use of red, particularly in Sada's kimonos, is a repeated theme, signifying the sexual warrior, amorous and dangerous.

This concept is emphasised as the sexual union is consummated and progresses. The *sake*, passed from mouth to mouth, presages Sada's "taking" nature; this is her first draining of Kichi's gifts. Eroticism explodes like a scarlet flower in the image of Kichi's erect penis. If the analogy of the *corrida* is to be sustained, here are the representations of the *banderillas* pricking the bull; the first orgasm quickly achieved by Sada – the *petite mort*, the first of many. Kichi already owes her a death.

"We have all the time in the world," says Kichi as Sada rushes to her orgasm (as if she subconsciously knows the untruth of this). She cements her claim by languorously fellating her new possession to a climax. She is enchanted by the beautiful phallus. It is Kichi in microcosm, in itself a *corpus*, and to have him she must exert her power over it.

The love-passages are subject to constant interruptions, which heighten the tension. The appearance of the amiable *geisha* presents a continuation of the scene; the shaft of the *samisen* played by her follows the line of the erect phallus. The spell is broken only temporarily.

Here no restrictions exist, moral or visual, although within the tiny room and behind the easily opened partitions, constant voyeurism is evident. However the growing suspicions and societal disapproval are joyfully disregarded.[5]

The use of colour actively illustrates Sada's emotional flux. She wears purple (the colour of passion and nobility – love and conquest have made her an aristocrat), and her murderous fantasy on seeing Kichi and his wife in coitus reveals a mindset of aggressive rightful ownership. Again the technique of light

and darkness is used to good effect; Sada is sent out into the cold and the dark to fetch water; love locked out.

In the rickshaw scene that follows, the besotted Kichi tastes the menstrual fluid of his mistress. Here the character of Spain can be loosely evoked: there, in mediaeval times, an infallible charm to ensure the fidelity of a lover was to feed him with menstrual blood. All this Kichi does without coercion, laying the foundation for his eventual and fatal surrender.

Sada has enchanted him with the beauty of her body. He wants to stroke, caress, kiss. His skin, however, incites her to biting him. She wishes literally to devour him, to cannibalise him, to own him absolutely.

The film progresses in a series of amorous encounters which incorporate a fateful dimension. Every embrace points us along a road of knives, a quest for some sexual Grail. Passion upon passion in the realm of the senses, scenes holding an extraordinary sweep of almost macabre beauty; the gathering *tsunami* of love, sex and death seen on the far horizon.

Oshima's lovers vent their feelings in "the little house – your home, my home". In the mock wedding Sada, wearing the yellow of the Japanese chrysanthemum, of liberty and joy, enters into a ritual of psychic pain, trembling at the enormity of fulfilment, for this is, in truth, her first emotional defloration. There is an allusion to Shakespeare's play within a play (as in *A Midsummer Night's Dream*) – the sexual molestation of a young girl, a surrogate for the physically experienced Sada; the subsequent post-orgiastic serenity signalling all is peace for the moment; the ancient, sinister, batwinged entertainer who sings of Winter and Spring, an analogy of the age difference between Kichi and Sada, of which Kichi is always conscious. (He is, however, young and virile enough to

warrant Sada's assaults).

In Sada's mind, the "wedding" is the catharsis. Meanwhile *geishas*, servants and jealous ill-wishers congregate malevolently; but a *tsunami* halts for no obstruction.

As the ownership of Kichi's phallus is that of Kichi himself, the member has become a thing of night-long worship, to be serenaded, caressed, played with, with the greatest tenderness, to be captured like a fugitive, even the urges of Kichi's bladder brushed aside, reprising an earlier scene when Kichi prevents Sada from relieving herself. The control has passed to her completely. "You need not call me 'Master' now".

When Sada confesses her concerns about her hypersexuality Kichi innocently remarks: "I hope it is incurable", becoming part of a *folie à deux*. There are constant subtle references to the gathering tragedy. Oshima directs the narrative in a strict linear exposition, casting interludes and side-issues in minor catalytic roles. Again he uses light and darkness as symbols of love and loss; Sada, leading Kichi by his penis (where others might merely hold his hand) takes him into a shadowy alcove where they copulate carelessly even when hailed by a washerwoman.

The masculine in Sada is revealed by a subtle intemperance and recklessness; she drinks *sake* from the bottle as she might drain a phallus. The red kimono (the *muleta* of the matador) underlines her possessiveness as, forcing him to wear it, she drapes it over Kichi's naked body like a premonition of blood. Completely proprietorial, she leaves him in the care of a maidservant, who warns him that Sada will be his death, and who is rewarded with rape for what he subconsciously recognises as an awesome truth.

Kichi is seen supine and unclothed, a prologue to the violence which Sada initiates with the old professor, a rehearsal which dispenses with respect (for death is no respecter of rank), and an anodyne to the pain she feels on separation

from Kichi whom she envisions in flight. When they are reunited it is against a background of huge black trains, ominously stationary as if poised to run the lovers down.

It is now behind a screen (the viewer is initially denied the full catharsis) that Sada mounts Kichi for the first time and initiates him into pain given and received. The feminine in him shrinks from violence, while she is all love and sharpness; even the jade ornament in her hair has a spiked point. At this juncture dialogue has become more or less redundant, subsumed in Kichi's willingness to accede to anything that gives her pleasure.

Her confession of beatings with the older lover is accepted with equanimity. She is the beloved mistress/master, *La Belle Dame Sans Merci*, the playful dominatrix, the frail, ivory-bodied Circe, Melusine, Eve, Lilith. She is older than the painted rocks behind La Giaconda, and childishly beautiful as a pre-Raphaelite virgin.

The foods she gives him, ripe from her vaginal juices, are all mystic sacraments of power and desire. The mushroom, when cooked, has the identical smell to semen; it is the Taoist sign of immortality and the food of the gods[6]. To the Chinese the fungus (*ling-chih*), symbolises the female sex organ[7], while the mushroom cloud above Hiroshima and Nagasaki is thought, paradoxically, to represent the phallic male principle.

By eating the egg from her vagina[8] he falls, mythologically, "into the

power of the witch". Sada gives birth to the fertility symbol and, witnessed by the death-white face of the doll-like *geisha*, she feeds Kichi with her offspring. In effect, the masculine Sada fertilises the feminine Kichi.

Using the device of a lamplit mirror in a darkened room, Oshima reveals the duplicity of Sada's emotion: the passionate affection against which the neurotic urge to possess her lover beyond all reason and sanity is laid; she threatens the penis with scissors, clearly stating her intention: "I am going to turn you into a skeleton."

Accepting his vow of fidelity and his acknowledgement of the penalty for its breaking: "I will allow you to kill me if I ever make love to my wife again," Sada/Delilah contents herself with a wisp of his pubic hair which she cannibalises.

In the dark and rain, Sada is safe under the shared umbrella, partners in *l'amour fou*, and unsuccessfully commands her "instrument" to rape a passerby whom they overpower and frighten. In an inn she taunts the patron with her sex, an affirmation of her power. Yet subsequently alone, the night reveals her misery, the rain mimics her tears. The small boy in the sauna receives the full venom of her thwarted desire as she pulls his penis. She hurts the male, "the tiny man", as she herself is hurting.

Kichi and Sada's indivisibility is profound. A dog barks at night as Kichi lies with his wife; an omen of the witch Hecate[9], who stands at the crossroads with power over land, sea and death. Blood flows as he cuts himself shaving and the wife, herself infected with the vampirism of love, seduces a body which no longer belongs to him or to her. A stone through the window denotes the warrior is at the gate.

There is an accelerated shift in the passion which assumes dimensions of such staggering potency that the viewer can easily suspend belief that these are mere theatricals. There is an authenticity to the violent erotic images possibly unequalled to date. Upon discovering the betrayal, Sada wields her knife (her warrior's phallus) with frenzied intent; the games are over. Previously Kichi has been almost an Oedipal figure, praising and envying Sada's youth. Now he is subjugated to the role of her puppet – "You undress me," while she holds the penis as if it were first her weapon and then an erring child whom she "punishes" with her body.

She takes responsibility for their situation; the claustrophobic, unclean, dimly-lit room is their enclave, the sanctuary where she keeps her treasure as a *samurai* hoards the spoils of a clan war. Still conscious of her honour which is now a joint entity with that of Kichi, she assaults the maid who complains of a disgusting odour, and once again instructs her living weapon to rape the girl. Only when an elderly *geisha* placates her does she hand out the favour of her lover's body, as if proud to show off his art. While they copulate, the camera fixes on Sada's naked body and wistful mouth as once again she shares an orgasm by proxy.

When Kichi sees the woman has wet herself, his innate vulnerability is revealed. "I thought I was holding my dead mother in my arms." A latent fixation is hinted at: the small boy who lives in all grown men perhaps revels in Sada's dominance, being reminded of past maternal discipline and tactility. Sada's own mother "suffered greatly before she died". For a moment there is a suggestion that what the lovers found in one another went through and beyond the sexual; a limitless mélange of dependence rooted in infancy: mother, father, child, lover, the whole ardently desired spectrum of physical comfort remembered and re-invented by the body's passionate chemistry.

Sada's statement: "I don't want our happiness ever to end," presupposes that possibility and fear is created. Subconsciously precognitive of tragedy of which she will be the joint architect, she seeks to avert it by appealing to the Oedipal figure of the professor to remove her temporarily from the scene. He betrays her by his refusal, excusing himself on the grounds of societal disapproval, though maybe recognising the dangers inherent in the passion with which she is psychically invested.

At the same time Kichi, a small, dark-clad figure, is seen isolated in a busy street where the army marches past between an honour guard of waving flags bearing the blood-coloured disc of the Rising Sun[10]. He sees the marching men as escapees from "civilised" life with its hazards, from the mirrored private invasion and combat which he undergoes through love. Psychologically emasculated for a moment by the sight of the warriors, he is a prisoner of love, already conquered, bound and sentenced.

In this brief scene Oshima reminds the viewer that there is another world out there, that there are things to come, outside the confined empire of the senses where a tumultuous force, more ancient than martial conquest, holds absolute autonomy.

Thus the lovers return to their appointed destiny; the *tsunami*, composed of love, passion, terror, longing, is closing over them; a half-recognised yet almost

cosmic ambition for total one-ness; a Calvary whose stations and implements are all artefacts of irresistible power; the power of sexual love, of a *petite mort* from which there can be no recovery.

Sada's frenzy, her fear of losing Kichi, is apparent. She is even jealous of his barber, she loves the nape of his neck (ready for the sword of *seppuku*?), her excitement when he shaves with a blade. He has become her property *in toto*, though the phallus is still representative of his entire physicality. Body and soul he is hers, to love, to cherish, to harm and injure, and to mourn and remember. He shares and owns her obsession; mentally and spiritually they are as much one as when they are joined in coitus.

Kichi will choose the manner of his death, the languid playful erotic strangling. He prefers it to the knife, for the knife is a false phallus and part of Sada's warrior persona, and her overwhelming feminine beauty must not be camouflaged by the brutality of steel. His death must be as languorous and protracted as their loving, with the orgasm of death constantly delayed. And when Sada binds his hands, it is not the crudity of fetishistic and careless bondage, but a loving restraint. Kichi is a full co-conspirator in this final act. The lovers are now both in the grip of a sublime insanity. The pain-play which he inflicts on her gives him no pleasure, for the feminine in him shrinks from hurting the lover/child/mother-figure which she represents.

Sada is also the goddess to be worshipped: the beautiful Morgan-le-Fay, the *Fata Morgana*, one of the Furies, a Valkyrie reaching from paradise. She is Kali, goddess of life and death, who wears a necklace of human skulls, who fertilises, who loves as she kills. She is the Japanese heroine of the Kabuki theatre, whose feminine attire and whitened mask conceal a powerful man.[11]

 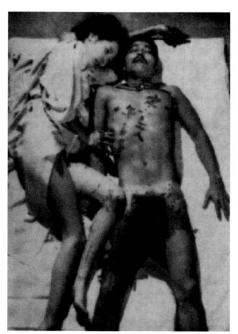

Oshima's final set implements both light and darkness, his vehicles for changing emotions of love, loneliness, desire and danger. The world outside has disappeared. There is only the room, dimly lit and highlighted by the silks on the floor, the yellow of liberation, the martial red of blood and passion. The scarf chosen for the execution is patterned in dark and light colours. The wavering screen, through which the viewer has fully penetrated, speaks of a coming moment of privacy, lunacy, sanctity. The sacrifice is laid out ready in his beauty. Music from the subtle *samisen* falls in a fugal torrent like water from a mountainside in oriental paintings. The *tsunami* rolls in to cover them both. Neither are responsible, for these lovers are mad.

In his wisdom, Oshima allows a candid image of the adored phallus slowly being received into the womb of the beloved. The lovers are one now, as much as they will ever be in life. The slow death-bringing is punctuated by the rising excitement of orgasm; the music blends with Sada's ecstatic cries and the dying breaths of her lover.

"I am bathing in a pool of red light!" This is the ultimate in possession, as the scarf tightens on his throat; with his death she buys him, and his willingness to please her by dying is the final witness of his love.

After the consummation Oshima gives us an extraordinary scene: Sada, enthralled and naked, lies alone on a park bench under a cold white sky, while a man and boy, who can be interpreted as Kichi, child and man, play hide and seek. They cry to one another in phrases which signify Kichi's departing soul. A sonorous drum-beat signals death. This scene is closely reminiscent of the shamanistic ritual in which, after sacrificing the beast, the drugged shaman links souls with his victim in trance[12].

The last scene of all is epic and monstrous.

Sada, mythical in her red kimono, stands over Kichi's body. She is the matador with his red *muleta* surveying the dead bull after the *corrida*. She is the priestess and the *samurai*. Her expressionlessness shows that she has reached for the impossible and attained it. Kichi is hers. No-one can ever have him again. One feels she would if she could devour him whole. Instead she takes her knife, her *descabello* used by a matador to administer the *coup de grâce*, and severs his penis, the emblem of love, the talisman of pleasure, the microcosmic Kichi, together with the seed-bearing testaments of generations not now to be born. The blood is mirrored by the kimono and stark against the white bodies. In her delicate hand she has the spoils of love and war. Where does she put them? Oshima's camera does not show us, but we know where. She puts them where they belong. The film itself seems to exhale a long breath of affirmation that Kichi and Sada are one for eternity.

The innate prudishness of Japanese cinema, which never balks at scenes of torture and bloodshed yet placed a ban on graphic sexuality, was a blessing in disguise for Oshima. His wisdom, intelligence and integrity was such that he was prepared to utilise the liberality of another country to realise his "pornography".

Without these hardcore scenes, the film would probably have ended up as hollow, sentimental, and possibly pretentious. What the film inspires is a visual truth, powerful almost beyond belief. It is in the exquisite explicit scenes, undoubtedly, profoundly and unarguably scenes of love and passion, that the film derives its *veritas* and potency. It is neither a question of taste nor sensationalism. What the viewer sees happening is a totally natural beauty – love demonstrated with humour, tenderness, savagery, and orchestrated by two exquisite beings who perform the sexual act with overwhelming grace and power. The honesty of the excitement (and this film is true erotica, arousing both the genitals and the psyche) which **Ai No Corrida** demonstrates is similar to discovering artwork such as the shockingly sublime imageries of a Hans Bellmer, or a Beardsley or a von Bayros.

At no time does the viewer feel manipulated by the sexual scenes. The viewer is a voyeur in the most intensive way, swept away into participation, enjoyment, and suffering, knowing that what he sees is the truth; an unsurpassed classic in the history of cinema. It is a majestic work which, because of its total openness and the refinements of its primitive beauty, goes almost beyond screen entertainment and certainly beyond most of today's erotica.

Oshima has translated a historical incident into a work of heroic legend. It is a living rather than a cinematic testament to Wilde's true maxim that "each man kills the thing he loves". It is a deep statement about the power of ageless, insane love, in which one soul jealously strives eternally to possess the other through the flesh.

It is a tale of loneliness, of insatiability, of hunger, of the phallus and the womb. It is Tristan and Isolde. It is tragedy. It is Lancelot and Guinevere, naked. It is the forbidden element of desire. It is Abelard and Héloise, Isis and Osiris. In this writer's view, it is that rarity, a masterpiece.

—Rosemary Hawley Jarman

*Noboru Tanaka's **True Story Of Sada Abe***

1 • Noboru Tanaka's **Jitsuroku: Abe Sada (The True Story Of Sada Abe)** was actually produced for Nikkatsu a year earlier, but is generally ignored in favour of Oshima's bigger-budget, international version of the same story. Tanaka's film features Junko Miyashita as Sada and Hideaki Ezumi as Kichizo.

2 • *The Samurai*, Jean Mabire and Yves Breheret. Wingate Press, London 1975.

3 • The *haiku*, from the *Imperial Verses* reads: "May we die/As in Springtime/The cherry tree flowers/Pure and lustrous" (*The Samurai*, Jean Mabire and Yves Breheret. Wingate Press, London 1975).

4 • *The Samurai*, Jean Mabire and Yves Breheret. Wingate Press, London 1975.

*Nagisa Oshima's **Ai No Borei***

5 • In Oshima's contrasting companion piece, **Ai No Borei (Empire Of Passion**, France/Japan, 1978), the lovers suffer in a climate of claustrophobic guilt and silence, damned by society, if only for their sexual crime – aside from the murder of the woman's husband. Here, Oshima retains a strict self-censorship, highlighting the transgression of the characters.

6 • *An Illustrated Encyclopaedia Of Traditional Symbols*, J.C. Cooper. Thames & Hudson, London 1988.

7 • *The Chinese Philosophy Of Time And Change – The Tao*, Philip Rawson and Laszlo Legeza. Thames & Hudson, London 1984.

8 • The insertion and removal of the egg from Sada's vagina is, coupled with the metaphor of the *corrida* or bullfight, the second reference to Georges Bataille's cataclysmic erotic novella *Story Of The Eye*. Kichi's final emasculation, echoing the castration of the priest in the novella, a third. Given that Bataille's fundamental assertion was that "eroticism is assenting to life, even in death", this would seem to be no coincidence.

9 • *Encyclopaedia Of Superstitions*, E & M.A. Radford and Christina Hole. Hutchinson, London 1974.

10 • This scene is almost certainly a reference to the notorious *ni-ni-roku* ("26 February") incident of 1936, which pre-dated the actual events of the Sada Abe case by only three months. On the morning of 26 February about 1,400 Japanese troops, under the command of junior officers seized the centre of Tokyo, executing a number of government officials. They declared they would not retreat until a new cabinet was established to implement sweeping reforms and social change. The rebels were intent on following through the writings of Ikki Kita, who in 1919 had published his *Nihon Kaizo Hoan Taiko* ("Outline Plan For The Reorganization Of Japan"). The government, acting on Imperial orders, initially acceded to their wishes but, after a few days,

Yoshishige Yoshida's **Martial Law**

reneged and declared martial law. Kita was executed a few days later for his part in the failed *coup d'état*. His life, and the *coup* itself, became the subject of Yoshishige Yoshida's film **Kaigenrai (Martial Law, 1973)**.

This incident was echoed in 1970 when Yukio Mishima, another Right-wing writer (author of *Confessions Of A Mask*, *The Man Who Fell From Grace With The Sea*, etc), led his private army the Society of the Shield in an attempted *coup* which led to Mishima's public *seppuku*. In turn, Mishima's 1965 film **Yukoku (Ritual Of Love And Death)** thematically prefigures **Ai No Corrida**.

Yukio Mishima's **Ritual Of Love And Death**

11 • Female roles in Japanese Kabuki theatre are traditionally played by male actors, known as *onnagata*, or *oyama*. This duality is perhaps best explored cinematically in Kon Ichikawa's **Yukinojo Henge (An Actor's Revenge, 1963)**, in which the eponymous female impersonator avenges the death of his parents by a complicated scheme of duplicities which function on many levels of opposition. The film's visual complexity is equally ingenious, as Ichikawa utilises notions of Kabuki to manipulate screen-space, perspective, lighting and characterisation. The tradition of cross-dressing persists, typified by transvestite lead actors Maruyama Akihiro in the ultra-camp **Kurotokage (Black Lizard, 1968)**, and Peter in Toshio Matsumoto's **Bara No Soretsu (Funeral Procession Of Roses, 1969)**. Peter's other roles range wildly from the Fool in **Ran** (1985, Akira Kurosawa's prestigious version of *King Lear*) to a mad bitch doctor in the trash video **Za Ginipiggu 5: Akuma No Joi-san (Guinea Pig 5: Devil Woman Doctor, 1992)** [see chapter 6].

*Peter (foreground) in Toshio Matsumoto's **Funeral Procession Of Roses***

Kabuki theatre was traditionally established in 1586 by the female temple dancer O Kuni, evolving over the next two hundred years to its present form, with male actors playing all the parts, and incorporating narrative elements of *bunraku* (puppet plays) and the earlier Noh theatre. Most notable mainstream film adaptations of Kabuki plays include Teinosuke Kinugasa's **Chushingura (The Loyal Forty-Seven Ronin, 1934)**, a version of *Kanadehon Chushingura*, first performed in 1748; Akira Kurosawa's **Tora No O O Fumu Otokotachi (Walkers On The Tiger's Tail, 1945)**, based on *Kanjincho*, first performed as Kabuki in 1810; and Kimisaburo Yoshimura's **Bijo To Kairyu (Beauty And The Dragon, 1955)**, a version of *Narukami* (1684). Perhaps the best avant-garde interpretation of a Kabuki play is Toshio Matsumoto's **Shura (Pandemonium, 1971)**, banned in the UK for its depiction of bloody infanticide. **Shura**

Akira Kurosawa's **Throne Of Blood**

derives from *Kamikaketa Sango Taisetsu* by Nanboku Tsuruya (1755–1829), also author of the oft-filmed Kabuki play *Yotsuya Kaidan* (*Ghost Story Of Yotsuya*), of which Nobuo Nakagawa's is the most celebrated cinematic version.

Noh theatre developed from travelling fairs, and its present form derives from the player Zeami Motokiyo (1362–1443). It is a highly stylized art form, relying on symbolism, allusion and body language to convey complex themes. Noh elements have rarely been incorporated into film, but two examples of note are Masaki Kobayashi's **Kwaidan**, a ghost story whose spectres all have Noh correlatives [see also chapter 6, note 7], and Akira Kurosawa's **Kumo No Su-Jo (Throne Of Blood,** 1957), his version of *Macbeth* which features a Noh chorus narrative, Noh stagings, and fetishized make-up resembling Noh masks.

12 • *Shaman*, Joan Halifax. Thames & Hudson, London 1982.

ABNORMAL WARD

THE SECRET CINEMA OF HISAYASU SATO

佐藤寿保

"I want to make a film which has the influence to drive its audience mad, to make them commit murder."

—Hisayasu Sato

TO this day – perhaps more so than ever before – the world of adult films remains the most opportune, if not the only, arena in which young Japanese film-makers can hone their craft whilst exploring their own personal visions and obsessions. In the last decade the pink *nouvelle vague* cinema has produced such experimental, innovative directors as Kazuhiro Sano, Toshiki Satoh, Takahisa Zeze and, most interestingly of all, Hisayasu Sato.[1]

In some ways, Hisayasu Sato is reminiscent of a modern-day Koji Wakamatsu; not just in his prolific output of movies (around 50 in just over a decade), but also in the controversial, provocative content of those works with their marriage of porno sub-culture to avant-garde expression. Working with regulars like writer Shiro Yumeno and actress Kiyomi Ito, Sato has produced a body of films – averaging in length to around 60 minutes – which are dedicated to exposing the dark void at the heart of contemporary existence. They brim with mute hysteria and deal with a violence of the soul that often erupts into the outside world. Films like **Exciting Ero: Atsui Hada (Exciting Eros: Hot Skin *aka* Gimme Shelter**, 1986); **Rorita Baibuzeme (Lolita: Vibrator Torture *aka* Secret Garden**, 1987); **Boko Honban (Rape: For Real *aka* Lustmord**, 1987); **Hard Focus Nusumigiki (Hard Focus: Wiretapping *aka* Survey Of Lost Paradise**, 1988); **Bijin Reporter: Boko Namachukei (Beauty Reporter: Live Hook-Up For Rape *aka* Love Obsession**, 1989); **Special Lesson Hentai Seikyoiku (Special Lesson: Perverted Sex Education *aka* Neurasthenic Gods**, 1990); **Mibojin Hentaijigoku (Widow In Pervert Hell *aka* Look Into Me**, 1991); **Seifuku Onanie Shojo No Shitagi (Masturbation In Uniform: Virgins' Panties *aka* Close Dance**, 1992); **Hitozuma Gomon Sandanzeme (Torture Of Married Women: The Three Steps *aka* Labyrinth Of Primary Colours**, 1992); **Mofukuzuma Teimo Nawa Dorei (Widow In Mourning: Shaven Rope Bitch *aka* Negation**, 1993); **Chikan To Nozoki Fujinkabyoto (Pervert And Peeping Tom: Gynaecology Ward *aka* Sick People**, 1994); **Hitozuma Hentaibiyoshi (Married Woman: Pervert Hairdresser *aka* Dead End**, 1994); and **Iyarashii Hitozuma (Horny Married Woman: Wet *aka* Love – Zero = No Limit**, 1995)[2].

Exciting Eros: Hot Skin

Films peopled by maniac rapists who explode their rage against women's bodies, who reside in darkened basements, mortuaries, container trucks, lightless tanks, porno cinemas. Women in schoolgirl sailor uniforms separated from reality by phobias, paranoia, suicidal impulses, narcolepsy, the melancholy of the exposed embryo; inhabiting a virtual world of white noise, blue screen, destructive desires and fatal madness. In **Hanrahonban: Joshi Daisei Boko-hen (Half-Naked Real Take: Raping Female University Students** *aka* **Rose Of Super Power,** 1989), a computer salesman turns rapist by night, attacking only women who live in white buildings; in **Hitozuma Collector (Married Woman Collector** *aka* **Rotten City,** 1985), a taxi driver is a gasmask-wearing rapist who victimizes his female passengers; and in **Chikandensha: Iyarashi Koi (Train Of Perversion: Dirty Actions** *aka* **Birthday,** 1994), a sociopathic pervert declares his utter divorce from reality. In **Boko: Climax (Rape: Climax** *aka* **Waters High,** 1986), the estranged female protagonist was born in a white cell without knowing her parents, while the heroine of **Hentaibyoto SM Shinryoshitsu (Abnormal Ward: S/M Consultation Room** *aka* **Alpha-Beta Fugue,** 1989) was separated from her identical twin by the scalpel of a strange doctor; and in **Seifukushikei: Nejirikome! (Private Torture Of Uniforms: Thrust It In!** *aka* **Just An Illusion,** 1990), a dissociated woman is pathologically unable to remove her school uniform. In **Hentaibyoto Hakuizeme (Abnormal Ward: The Torture Of White Dresses** *aka* **Love Letter In Sand,** 1988), a nurse cannot touch the button of her elevator without repeatedly disinfecting it; she becomes attached to a young girl who was raped on a rainy day, to the point where she inherits the girl's experience and, when it rains, beats men to death at random with a metallic bat. Though she has no memory of her actions, every night she screams hysterically into a hole made in a water tank full of sand.

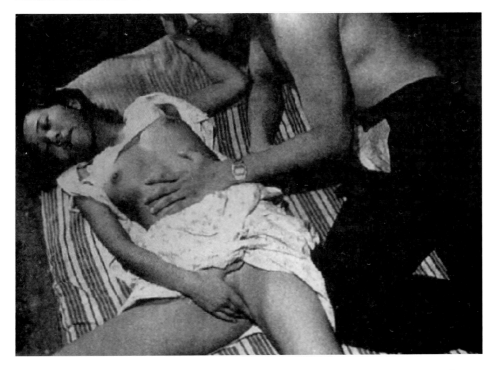

Married Woman Collector

Rape: Climax

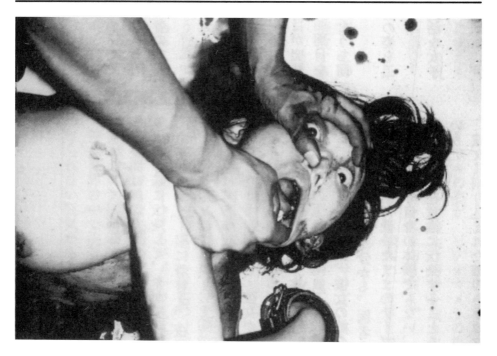

Lolita: Vibrator Torture

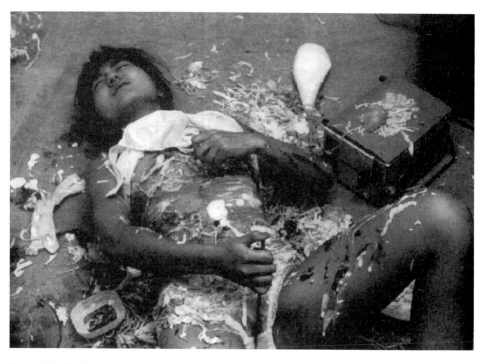

Rape: For Real

Hard Focus: Wiretapping

Abnormal Ward: S/M Consultation Room

Beauty Reporter: Live Hook-Up For Rape

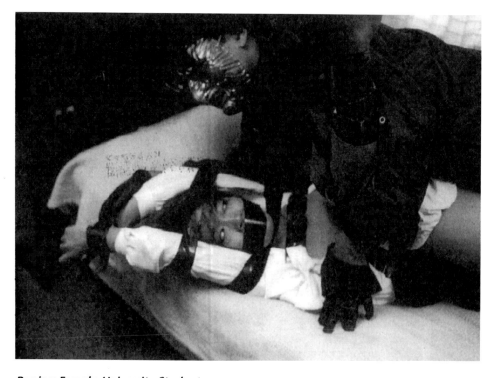

Raping Female University Students

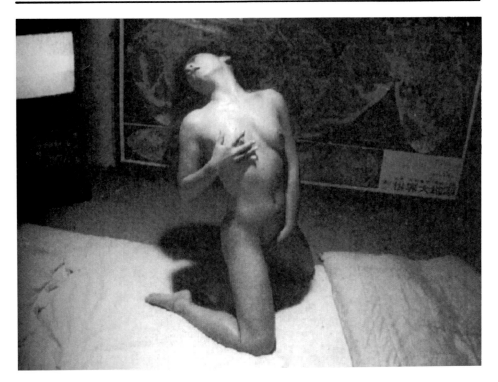

Special Lesson: Perverted Sex Education

Private Torture Of Uniforms: Thrust It In!

Masturbation In Unifom: Virgins' Panties

Torture Of Married Women: The Three Steps

Married Woman: Pervert Hairdresser

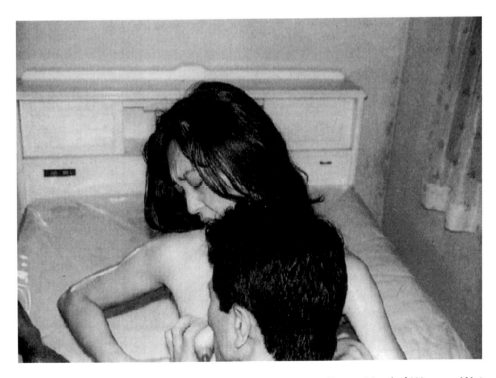

Horny Married Woman: Wet

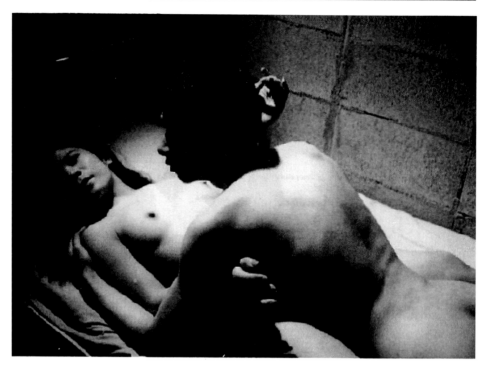

Hidden Filming Report: Sneak Shots aka Turtle Vision

Two typical Sato films are **Tosatsu Report: Insha!** (Hidden Filming Report: Sneak Shots *aka* Turtle Vision, 1991) and **Uwakizuma Chijokuzeme** (Unfaithful Wife: Shameful Torture *aka* An Aria For The Eyes *aka* The Bedroom, 1992). **Turtle Vision** opens with a sequence of secretly-shot, voyeuristic video images. Eiji (played by Koichi Imaizumi), a young cameraman, makes his living by filming these tapes and selling them to the porn industry. He is a solitary person who lives alone in a dark loft and has no outside contacts save for those he sells his tapes to. One night, while filming, he discovers a prostitute in a schoolgirl's sailor uniform (Rei Takagi) working the backstreets of Okubo, and secretly follows her with his camera. The girl leads a middle-aged man to a deserted building site, where she lets him grope her body as he likes. Suddenly, she pulls out a concealed knife and stabs her client viciously in the eyes. The man collapses and writhes in agony, blood pouring from his eye-sockets. Fascinated, Eiji decides to pursue this weird girl wherever she goes.

We learn that her name is Saki; she lives a bizarre double life as a cheerful high school student by day, disturbed prostitute by night. Saki lives in a flat with her elder sister, Maki. Maki seems equally strange; she never leaves home, sitting all day with drawn shutters, wearing dark sunglasses. She never speaks and her face remains blank, inscrutable, even when Saki tells her about her day at school. One night, as they sleep side by side, Maki is tormented by an unknown nightmare; Saki awakes abruptly, dresses in her sailor uniform and heads off into the night. Once again she lures a man to a lonely spot then mutilates his eyes.

One night, after a similar attack on a client, Saki appears to fall down unconscious. Eiji, who has been filming, aids her and finds she is in a somnambulistic state; she can later remember nothing of her actions. Eiji takes her to a psychiatrist who probes her subconscious, eventually locating the imprint of a trauma which Saki has apparently inherited from her sister Maki, as if by psychic infection. The trauma is revealed to have occurred when Maki was a high school student. Her boyfriend at the time was filming her one day with his video camera, when a group of thugs disguised in stocking masks appeared and attacked them. The boyfriend was knocked unconscious, and Maki was viciously gang-raped in a prolonged assault. Halfway through her ordeal her boyfriend came around, but was too scared to help her, averting his gaze; then, inexplicably, he picked up his camera and began compulsively to film the brutal rape. Maki, who by now was resigned to her fate, turned hysterical upon seeing the camera, endlessly screaming "No, no!!". This was the root of her eye-trauma, and the story also has shocking repercussions for Eiji: he realises *he* was the boyfriend! And thus his own fetish, his voyeurism, was born; seeing himself powerless to help Maki, he became detached from the exterior world, his only way of communicating with it now being through a video lens.

Having come to turns with the past, Eiji returns to the scene of the crime. Maki, dressed in her sailor uniform, awaits him on the highschool roof. They embrace, then ritualistically slice open each other's eyes; both die in cathartic streams of blood. Saki, left alone, still bears the traumatic imprint. Soon after, we see her wandering the streets; caught in the cyclopean gaze of a video camera she erupts, slashing at the camera's lens with her knife. Fade to white noise.

In **Turtle Vision**, Sato presents one of his main themes: the persistence of madness – as a ghostly imprint on the minds of others – even after its source has been destroyed. Two people, fatally detached from the world by trauma, are able to mutually terminate their psychosis in a bloody tryst, yet this insanity lives on in the scream of one close to them. Finally, as Saki's knife swipes at the video lens, it is the voyeuristic eyes of the film's audience that are also in danger of mutilation. Sato's films often end with a switch to white noise and the signal "GAME OVER", reinforcing the virtual nature not only of the cinematic experience, but of our relationship to "reality" and the exterior world itself. Perhaps traumatised by his images, the audience emerge warily from the dark of the porno cinema as their eyes are stabbed by the blinding white light of day.

The Bedroom opens with a shot of a video camera lens being spray-painted black. Thus commences another libidinal psychodrama in which the identities of two sisters are intertwined, leading to murder and madness. This time the film centres around a sect of alienated young people who use/abuse a narcotic called Halcion and frequent The Bedroom, a dark cell lit only by a huge video screen of silent static. Here, girls take sleeping pills and lie naked on a bed while various men photograph, grope, explore and penetrate their comatose bodies. Kyoko is one such girl, whose younger sister Maya has just been found dead, wrapped from head to foot in cling-film, next to an empty bottle of Halcion. Kyoko's husband, Esaka, is devoid of love for her and can only communicate by abusive sex; Kyoko is now involved in an affair with Kei, her sister's former boyfriend. They make love blindfolded, under ultra-violet light. Kyoko keeps a compulsive video diary of her life, which is punctuated by bizarre hallucinations/flashbacks and a growing phobia of surveillance cameras, presumably the result of Halcion use. (She likens the drug to a feeling "like Spring was put to an end by death" – presaging the rainy season – its very name evoking *haru-shi-on*, the Japanese characters for Spring, death, sound.)

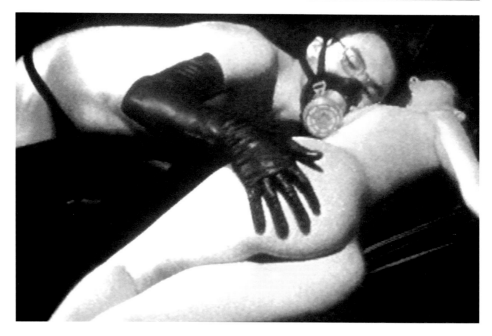

Unfaithful Wife: Shameful Torture aka *The Bedroom*

Kyoko starts using the Bedroom without taking the sleeping pills, staying conscious – but never opening her eyes – while men in gasmasks and latex probe her nude body. On one visit, she and her friend discover a dead girl in the Bedroom, killed by an overdose of Halcion. She also discovers that her lover Kei is a long-term Halcion user. Kyoko's hallucinations start to include herself being videoed, naked, by her mother. Her relationship with Kei descends into video delirium. She stares into the watching lens as they fuck, anamorphic close-ups of her nipples and Kei's tongue flashing on-screen; she films her own genitals as she masturbates, and the TV relays each detail to Kei; they film each other, closer and closer, until the lenses of their cameras clash in a cold kiss. On Kyoko's next visit to the Bedroom, she opens her eyes for the first time as she is fondled, and is horrified to see that the man is Kei, wearing the dark glasses of a blind man and apparently in a narcoleptic trance state.

Meanwhile, another girl is found dead in the Bedroom, her metallic-painted body viciously striped with knife-tracks. Kyoko asks Mr Takano, the master of the Bedroom seen only via a distorted image in the video screen, whether he is responsible for her murder (ever the provocateur, Sato gave the role of Mr Takano to cannibal killer Issei Sagawa[3]). When she returns to Kei's flat, she finds him comatose next to a near-empty bottle of Halcion. Finding a video he has made, she watches it. It shows a terrified girl being chased, about to be raped, from the camera-user's point-of-view; Kyoko realises that Kei must be the killer. She revives him, he drowsily calls her Maya. She stabs him in the neck, cuts open her own hand. As Kei lies dying on the floor, she stuffs the rest of the Halcion into his mouth. "Me or my sister – which one did you love?". As Kyoko tries to push Kei's body into the fridge, Mr Takano arrives. He claims that she is his wife, and shows her surveillance recordings of her visits to the Bedroom which reveal

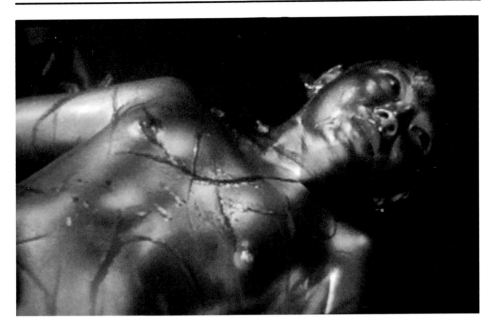

Unfaithful Wife: Shameful Torture aka *The Bedroom*

Unfaithful Wife: Shameful Torture aka *The Bedroom*

that *she* is the killer. She is in fact the younger sister Maya – it is Kyoko who has died, overdosed on Halcion; her death has traumatised Maya, confusing her identity, driving her to take more and more pills, to become paranoid of gazes. "That day, the world entered the rainy season. Everything that is surrounded by the capsule of endless falling water is dissolving. The earth... the cities... me..."

Woman Abuse: Naked Blood

The film terminates with a bizarre coda, Kyoko's suicide by cling-film viewed in reverse, as the disembodied voice of Takano welcomes her back from the dead. END scrolls upscreen. With **The Bedroom**, Sato has produced another stylish composition of complex intercuts, flashbacks, recurring images, traumas, violence, hallucinations and perverse eroticism. Once more it is the camera's persistent gaze which punctuates the lives of his protagonists, as they struggle under the melancholy of subliminal manias and blurred identity, submerging the viewer by degree into the director's addictive, tactile pessimism.

Perhaps the most extreme and bewildering of Sato's recent films is **Nyogyaku NAKED BLOOD (Woman Abuse: Naked Blood**, 1996), in which the director on one hand takes a noticeable step away from sex cinema towards a more mystical plane, yet on the other encompasses along the way some of the most gruelling and graphic scenes of mutilation ever committed to film. As in **The Bedroom**, the premise of **Naked Blood** hinges on the invention of a new psychotropic drug. Eiji, a seventeen-year-old student, has developed a stimulant named Myson, a "pure anaesthesia" which by promoting the mass secretion of endorphins can literally turn pain into pleasure. At the same time his mother, a doctor, is conducting research into a new form of contraceptive medicine. Eiji secretly injects Myson into the contraceptive drips, and the three young girls taking part in an experiment to test the birth control drug are unwittingly dosed with his revolutionary pain-killer. Eiji videotapes the experiment from an adjoining rooftop; one of the girls, Mikami, sees and watches him.

We later learn that all three girls have their own eccentricity; one is obsessed with eating, another is a narcissist, and Mikami herself suffered such a trauma on the occasion of her menarche that ever since that day she has been unable to sleep. Mikami lives in a stark white, antiseptic apartment which also

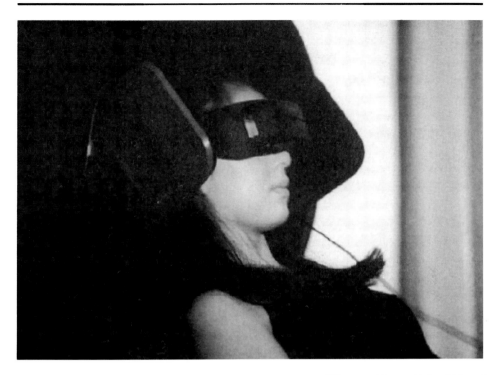

Woman Abuse: Naked Blood

contains a giant, silver cactus which she talks to. She also links to it "telepathically" via VR headsets wired to the plant and to her black leather sleep simulation chair. In this way Mikami experiences how the cactus feels and dreams of desert landscapes; but she is also plagued by vivid menstrual nightmares which place her in overlit arcades, her whole body and school uniform drenched in catamenial blood, the only escape a swimming-pool which forever clouds with crimson.

Watching videotapes of his mother's experiment, Eiji becomes obsessed with Mikami as she stares into his lens; he starts to follow her around, filming her, until she confronts him. She takes Eiji to the botanical gardens, a place which she hates despite its beauty, since due to her hypersensitive hearing she is virtually deafened by the "screaming of the flowers" and the indecipherable chatter of insects. This, Mikami confides, makes her suicidal. They adjourn to the tranquillity of her apartment (the "dormant" cactus, she explains, is the only silent plant), where Eiji tries the VR headset and soon "sees" an oceanic dreamscape.

The film now intercuts between the other two girls who took part in the experiment, and Eiji's mother. One girl, the narcissist, examines her body in the mirror. Plucking a stray hair from her armpit, she is surprised that this normally painful act feels somehow pleasurable. She then pierces her ears with needles, beginning to revel in the sensation. Meanwhile the other girl, the glutton, cuts her thumb while preparing *tempura*, and sucks on it with greedy pleasure. She is soon compelled to thrust her batter-coated hand into hot oil, feeling no pain, and then starts to chew on her own cooked fingers in auto-cannibalistic ecstasy. The Myson is taking effect...

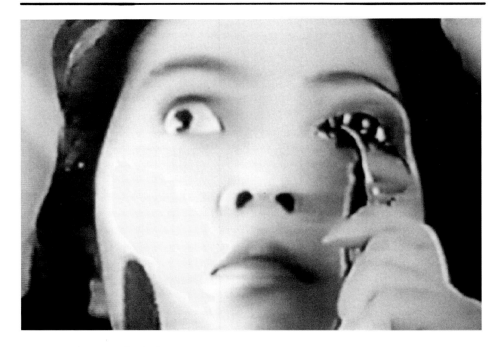

Woman Abuse: Naked Blood

Eiji's mother is watching old Super-8 films of herself and her late husband. A beach scene, she is pregnant with Eiji. Her husband sees a "flash of light" on the horizon, wades out into the sea to investigate and suddenly, in the blink of an eye, is gone forever. We later learn that he was a scientist researching into immortality, by means of the transmogrification of mortal mass into light.

Cut to the narcissist, who by now has punctured nearly her entire body with safety-pins, bodkins and even the thick, sharpened awl which we now see her driving in and out of her forearm. Her entire skin is blood-drenched and hanging with silverware, her compulsive pleasure at this self-perforation almost orgasmic. Cut back to the glutton, for what is surely the most bizarre and gut-wrenching sequence of self-mutilation ever shown in a commercial film. She is naked, sitting on the kitchen table, and slowly, deliberately, eating herself with a knife and fork. Starting with the erogenous zones, she cuts off her own vaginal lips and devours them, raw and bloody; next comes her nipple, sliced clean off, and then she plunges the fork into her own eyeball, extricates it roots and all, and chews it deliriously while her empty socket weeps cataracts of crimson[4].

The next time we see the narcissist she is dead, a six-inch awl stuck through her forehead into her brain, victim of the ultimate piercing. Likewise the glutton, who lies lifeless on her kitchen table in a veritable ocean of blood. Eiji's mother, learning of their deaths, is understandably distraught; she analyses her contraceptive drug and discovers traces of Myson. Eiji admits his deceit and rushes away. The doctor calls Mikami to the hospital, and finds alarming levels of endorphins in her bloodstream. We next see Mikami leaving the hospital to join Eiji, who has cycled to her apartment. Cut to Eiji's mother, who now lies immobile, barely alive, on a bed in the experiment room; her abdomen has been cut wide open, the skin and muscle peeled back to expose her pulsating viscera. Eiji is filming from the next rooftop.

Eiji injects himself with the remaining Myson, and he and Mikami don the VR headsets. "The dream will live inside us forever." They fuck in virtual space, naked bodies entwined over psychedelic backdrops of purple cacti, overlit clinical wards, vast oceanic/maternal spaces[5]. In flashback we see Mikami visiting and dispatching her two colleagues: plunging the awl into the narcissist's head, repeatedly stabbing the glutton with a butcher knife till her blood sprays out in fountains. Next she is seen vivisecting Eiji's mother with a scalpel, opening up her belly, tearing apart the skin and stomach walls.

Mikami and Eiji cease copulating, remove the VR sets. Mikami pulls out a retractable blade and slashes Eiji's throat, repeating the act with savage violence till his blood spurts in geysers. As he expires, we cut to the hospital where his mother has a dying vision of her late husband. He climbs head first into her gaping abdomen, disappearing completely inside her, and pulls closed the flaps of skin and muscle behind him. She dies, her body dissolves into light. Cut back to Mikami's apartment – her dormant cactus has flowered. Fade to white screen.

A brief coda shows Mikami several years later, a nomad accompanied by the young son she conceived with Eiji (also named Eiji and already weaned onto his first video camera), on a mission to defoliate the planet of all plant life except the cactus. "The dream will never be over."

Mixing shock gore effects with cybersex, medical fetishism, video mediation, narcolepsy and Nietzschean notions of eternal return, **Naked Blood** may well be the ultimate fusion of the visceral, the psychopathological and the metaphysical, a film whose nearest analogue in Western cinema would be the work of David Cronenberg[6]. Hisayasu Sato's *oeuvre* is fast becoming equally, if not more, disturbing than Cronenberg's, and although his films lack the latter's technical polish – primarily as a result of budgetary limitations – his future directions threaten to lead the viewer into uncompromising, hitherto uncharted realms of venereal psychosis and virtual delirium.

NOTES

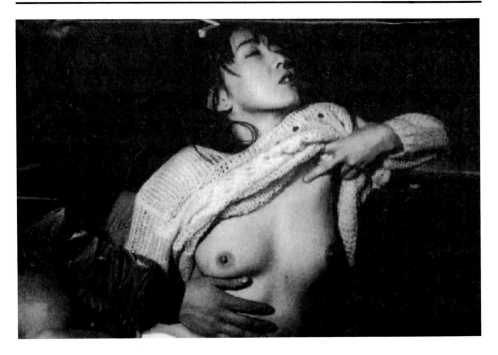

Charge! Lolita Poaching

1 • In fact these directors are known as the "Pink Shitenno" ("Pink Best 4"), and their films are highly regarded. Hisayasu Sato was born 1959 in Shizuoka City, and graduated from Tokyo College of Industrial Arts to become an assistant director at Shishi Productions. After working for various directors he made his solo debut in 1985 with **Totsugeki! Rorita Mitsuryo (Charge! Lolita Poaching** *aka* **Mad Sensation)**. For this and two other films he directed the same year – **SEX Otometai: Kemonotachi No Utage (Sex Virgin Team: Banquet Of Beasts** *aka* **Zero Flight)** and **Married Woman Collector** – he won the prize for Best New Director at the pink film industry's annual Zoom-Up Festival. Since then he has produced around 50 adult films, as well as a number of AV productions including **Bondage Collector: Kyonyugari (Bondage Collector: Big Tits Hunt, 1991); Mugen FUCK Jigoku (Boundless Fuck Hell, 1991); Inju No Tenshi (Angel Of The Filthy Beast, 1994)**; and **Mangekyo Binikunaburi (Kaleidoscope: Torture Of Beautiful Flesh, 1994)**.

2 • All Sato's films have double – seemingly unrelated – titles. **Kyrie Elesion**, for instance, is the other title of **Nama Tocho Report: Chiwa (The Live Bugging Reports: Dirty Talk); Uma To Onna To Inu (Horse, Woman, Dog)** is also known as **Beach Of Poaching**; the original title of **Kurutta Butokai (Mad Ball)** is **Ostia: Lunar Eclipse Cinema**, etc etc. This is typical of films by the Pink Best 4.

3 • In 1981 Issei Sagawa, the son of a wealthy Japanese businessman, was 32 and putting the finishing touches to his doctoral thesis in Paris. Sagawa, "a clever and delicate young man", became obsessed with a fellow postgraduate student, a 25-year-old Dutch woman named Renée Hartevelt. On June 11th 1981, Sagawa invited Hartevelt around to his apartment for dinner and a discussion about literature. After the discussion, Sagawa asked Hartevelt if she would have sex with him. After she

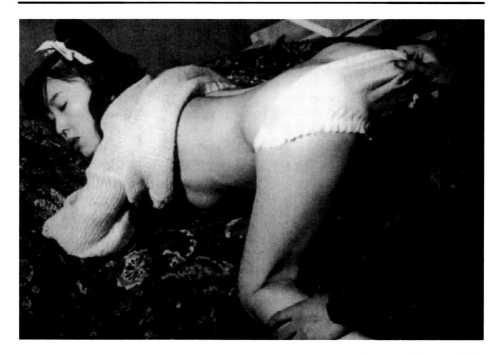

Charge! Lolita Poaching

declined, he requested that she read a poem into a tape recorder for him to work on his pronunciation. While she was doing so, Sagawa went to get his .22 calibre rifle and shot Hartevelt in the back of her head. He then had sex with her body, slept with it and ate portions of it raw. Two days later, he stuffed the remains of the body into a pair of suitcases which he dumped in the Bois de Boulogne, where they were soon discovered by the police.

When they raided Sagawa's small Paris apartment, police officers found pieces of red meat carefully wrapped in plastic bags, which were taken to the police laboratory. Forensic evidence established beyond any doubt that this was human flesh, cut from Hartevelt's arms, thighs and hips. Other pieces of human flesh in the refrigerator were eventually identified as coming from the victim's lips. These pieces matched the strange mutilations found on Renée Hartevelt's dismembered corpse.

Arrested and tried, Sagawa was found to be insane and committed to a French mental hospital. In May 1984 his father's company, Kurita Water Industries, signed an important business deal with the French chemical conglomerate Elf-Aquitaine, and, not accidentally, at the same time, Sagawa was transferred to a mental hospital in Japan. In August 1985 he was released from care, even though many doctors – including the hospital's deputy superintendent – considered Sagawa to be an untreatable psychotic.

Other notable Japanese killers of the modern era have included Tsutomu Miyazaki, an impotent paedophile "vampire" who in 1989 mutilated and murdered four schoolgirls and wrote odes to the body parts he kept in jars beneath the floorboards. Miyazaki was an avid collector of videos – he had around 6,000 of them – including such splatter/gore films as the notorious **Guinea Pig 2** [see chapter 6]. As a result, sale of certain videos in Japan was at last restricted to those aged over 18.

4 • In its prolonged and detailed presentation of these horrendous autophagous acts, **Naked Blood** goes almost as far in the gore stakes as other Japanese films such as

Guinea Pig 2 or **Atrocity** [see chapter 6].

5 • The ocean, swimming-pools, pools of blood, are a recurring maternal motif in the film. Eiji's mother even describes Myson (*my son*) as being "the colour of the sea".

6 • Cronenberg's films need no introduction. **Naked Blood** might be most closely compared to **Videodrome** (1983), while the themes of Sato's other films echo both the sibling traumas of **Dead Ringers** (1988) and the sex/technology interface most cogently expressed in **Crash** (1996).

ULTRAVIOLENCE

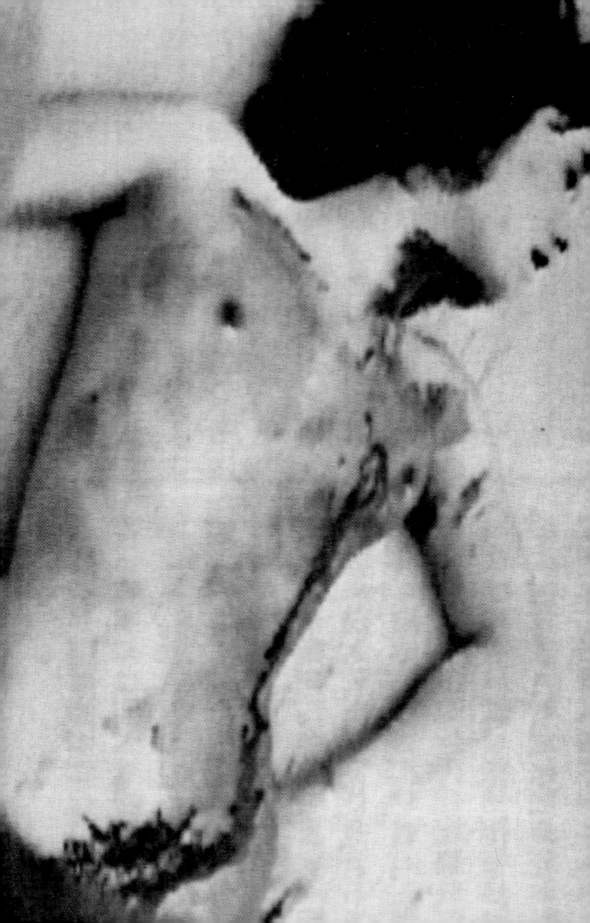

SEX, SLAUGHTER, SACRIFICE

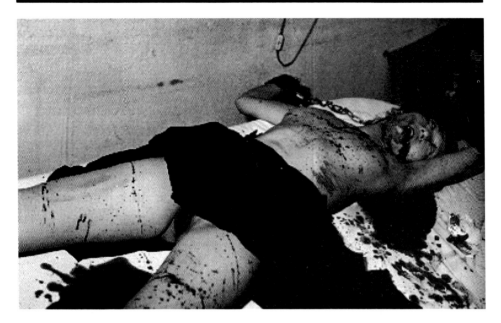

Hisayasu Sato's **Lolita: Vibrator Torture**

FROM the humiliation, torture and rape of women to misogynistic murder is a very small step, as already evidenced in the more extreme moments of Hisayasu Sato's **Naked Blood**, as well as other of his films such as **Lolita: Vibrator Torture**. But the killing of women is most notoriously – and most graphically – presented in the short, shot-on-video movies **Za Ginipiggu: Akuma No Jikken (Guinea Pig: Devil's Experiment, 1988)** and **Za Ginipiggu 2: Chiniku No Hana (Guinea Pig 2: Flower Of Bloody Flesh, 1989)**. **Devil's Experiment,** in its lurid packaging and presentation, gives the superficial impression that it might be a genuine "snuff" movie, a "semi-documentary film about a human lab-rat... a super-real raw movie"; the video box bears no production credits but asks "3 men torture a woman – is this an experiment?". The blurb goes on to promise "violence – screaming – intolerance – cruelty – horror... abuse, one hundred slaps, kicking, facial disfigurement, bleeding from the mouth, horrible pain... boiling oil poured onto arms, limbs mutilated, maggots in blisters, guts, insane screams, fingernails ripped off, eyeballs pierced by a pin". While this quite accurately sums up the video's 43-minute content, upon viewing it almost immediately becomes apparent that **Devil's Experiment** is no snuff movie but a professional, well-crafted cinematic exercise; its makers utilising such techniques as slow-motion, freeze-frame, fades, intercuts, overhead shots, point-of-view shots, close-ups, anamorphs, rapid-fire editing, captioning and sound-tracking in its composition. **Devil's Experiment** is, in fact, an effective and surprisingly low-key meditation on the cumulative dehumanization that violence causes in both aggressor and victim alike.

      Devil's Experiment opens with a disclaimer alleging that the video was received from an anonymous source, its makers and participants unknown, as if to propagate the illusion of it being a genuine snuff movie. The film itself then opens with washed-out, slightly grainy intercut images of a speeding roadside and

Guinea Pig 1

a slowly spinning white net, hung from a garden tree – images which, with hindsight, we realise represent the start and finish of a young girl's journey into living hell. Sparse background music accompanies a final close-up of the net, revealing its contents to be a corpse. Cut to title caption – "GUINEA PIG" – followed by the year of production, shown cryptically as "198X". Another caption appears, announcing the nature of the abuse to come – these captions appear throughout, each preceding a new segment of torture. The next image shows a girl's ankles being tied to a chair; then shutters are drawn, the room grows dark. We see the girl, dressed in a white dress, who as yet appears relatively unperturbed by her plight, and then her three captors who are dressed in black and wear dark glasses; two hold her while the third repeatedly slaps her face with a leather-gloved hand. The number 50 comes up at bottom screen right, indicating the total blows to date. Her assailant rubs salt into her bruised face, continues his assault. Fade to later; the girl's face is now noticeably more livid and swollen. The man pours coins into a leather bag, begins to pummel her jaw with this. 100 blows. She spits thick dark blood; fade to new caption. Blindfolded, hands tied, the girl is thrown to the floor and kicked repeatedly by all three men, who mutter obscenities. She tries to get up but is tripped, kicked again, then held and punched. Fade to next caption. We see her from overhead, clamped into some kind of black dentist's chair. Metal pincers pinch the skin on her hand, twisting. She gasps and whimpers, the pincers move up to her forearm and continue to pinch and twist cruelly. Fade to an outdoor shot, her body turning in its net; then in close-up, then an accelerating point-of-view shot from *inside* the net, which melts into a p.o.v of the girl as she is spun round and round in a swivel chair. The screen indicates 50 revolutions. Cut back to garden scene, back to 100 revs. Now a bottle of bourbon is poured down the disoriented girl's throat, the spinning continues; fade to later, she is wailing, drunk and hopelessly dizzy. 200 revs; she vomits everywhere. Fade to next caption.

A tape machine is switched on, emitting a loop of white industrial noise. The girl, tied in a chair, is fitted with headphones which are roped in place, the rope also gagging her. She moans drunkenly, rocks in the chair as her eardrums are brutally assaulted. Fade to later, she is squirming and screaming quite hideously. 5 hours of aural torture. Fade to 10 hours; the headphones are now gaffer-taped in place, the girl appears comatose, sightless, gurgling. A thick, grey-white drool pours from the corner of her slack mouth. Fade to next caption. The girl, viewed from above, is roped to bannisters. Two men pull at her hair and a fingernail with pliers; first a swathe of hair is torn out by the roots then, in close-up, the fingernail. Freeze-frame as the nail detaches from the raw fingertip. Cut to the garden, windswept, birds singing, a bleached shot of the white net slowly swinging; fade to next caption. We see a pan of hot oil simmering, then the girl who is outstretched on a black PVC sheet on a bed, hands roped tight above her head. A man pours the hot oil over her right arm. Cut to him returning with more oil, and the screen shows its temperature: 150 degrees. As he pours it over her arm again, we hear her grunts of pain and the sizzle of flesh. Hideous blistering is shown on the girl's skin. Fade to next caption. Then a close-up of writhing maggots. The girl is still tied to the bed as the maggots are sprinkled over her burnt arm and start to burrow into the raw wound. Then more maggots are dropped on her face as she lies twitching and barely conscious, the white grubs crawling in her eyes and mouth, her hair, then more over her legs. Close-up of the raw blister, maggots all over the suppurating flesh. Fade to next caption. Now the girl is being pelted with bucketfuls of raw offal, the bloody guts clinging to her face and torso as her captors snicker obscenely. When she is covered in entrails

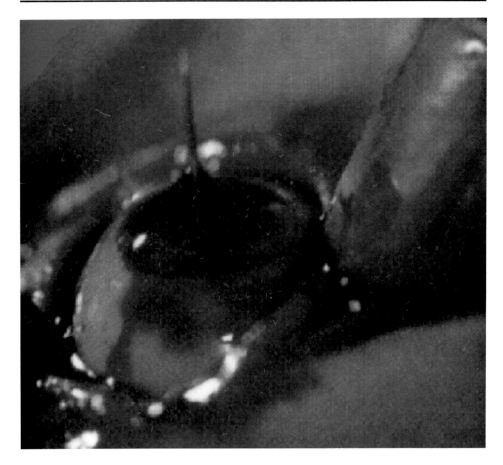

Guinea Pig 1

she finally awakes and, realising her plight, starts up with a series of piteous howling screams, as if this latest humiliation is the worst so far. Slow-motion shot of the offal arcing towards her, the men's mocking laughter distorting, echoing and ebbing away. Cut to the offal-covered bed, the ropes in place but the girl gone. Fade to garden. One of the men is raising a trip hammer over the body of the girl as it hangs in the net. Cut to close-up of her hand being sliced wide open with a scalpel. The hammer falls toward the net/cut to it landing on the lacerated hand, crunching bone. Fade to next caption. The bloodied girl is now gagged, tied in a chair, seemingly unconscious. From overhead we see one of her captors sharpening a long metal nail on an electric grinder. After a fair while, he hands the needle-like nail to his accomplice. The girl's head is jerked back and secured by a chain around the throat, her left eye held open. The needle is pushed into her cheek to the side of the eye; in close-up we see dark blood start to well up in the eye-socket. Cut to a concatenation of flash-frames showing glimpses of the previous tortures, then back to the girl's eyeball virtually submerged in blood. More flashbacks, then the needle finally bursts through the iris and cornea. Freeze-frame. Fade to a final shot of the girl's body in the net, slowly spinning, upside-down, melancholy in the washed-out light of a monumental evening. The

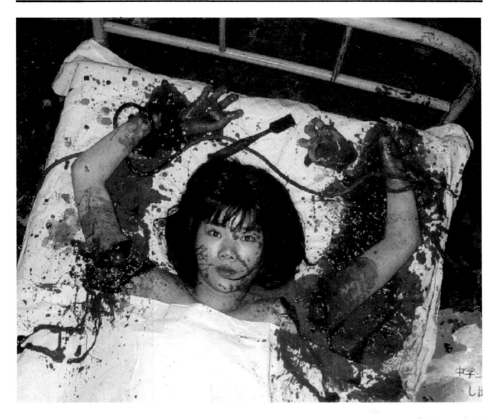

Guinea Pig 2

camera pulls away to distance; black-out. An end text reiterates the anonymity of the video recording, assures us that all efforts are being made to identify the dead girl.

After watching **Devil's Experiment** the viewer is left brutalised, undoubtedly, but also with that intangible sadness at the evanescence of human life which lies at the heart of much Japanese art.

The sequel to **Devil's Experiment, Flower Of Bloody Flesh**, makes no pretence at snuff authenticity, openly touting itself on the video box as the first film directed by *manga* artist Hideshi Hino[1]. The blurb goes on to promise a "shocking, grotesque world of blood, a scandalous splatter film with cutting-edge SFX and visual techniques"[2]. The video opens with a psycho dressed in a *samurai* outfit pursuing a young girl down night streets. He captures her and she wakes up tied to a bed. The psycho proceeds to drug, mutilate, maim, torture, dismember and disembowel her in graphic and quite convincing detail, muttering bizarre dialogue all the while, and finishing up by gouging out one of her eyes and eating it. His quest for the bloody "red flower" is (temporarily) satisfied. The psycho's lair is revealed to be full of grisly trophies from similar murders, and the film ends with him stalking yet another new victim[3]. **Flower Of Bloody Flesh** remains one of the most relentless and extreme gore films ever made, yet its ritualised excesses[4] are perhaps, ultimately, less disturbing or affecting than the cool, almost casually detached brutality and amorality of **Guinea Pig 1**.

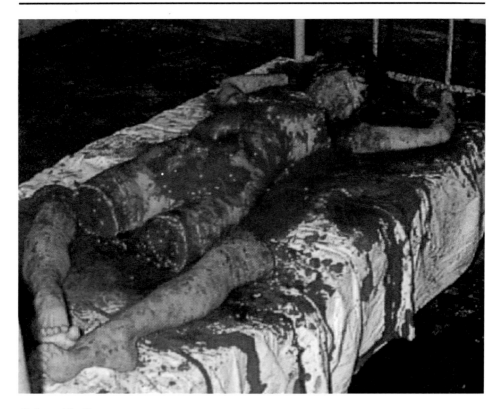

Guinea Pig 2

After these two entries, the **Guinea Pig** series quickly degenerated and the subsequent films are of little interest.[5] They have more in common with Izo Hashimoto's **Shiroi Kabe No Kekkon (Lucky Star Diamond** *aka* **LSD** *aka* **Bloody Fragments On White Walls,** 1989) – a film often, in fact, erroneously catalogued as being part of the **Guinea Pig** collective. As its English title suggests, **LSD** is the depiction of a harrowing and bloody bad acid trip. Yoko, the unfortunate user, has been confined to a treatment clinic, but continues to experience terrifying hallucinations. Driven hysterical by visions of maggots in her drip bottle, offal dangling from the ceiling, blood pouring down the walls, and finally her own entrails exploding in a welter of blood from her vagina, Yoko is sedated by her sister and a sinister doctor. Next, the doctor is performing brain surgery on Yoko, opening her skull with a power drill; a cockroach scuttles across the exposed cerebral cortex, and the doctor eats it alive while the sister, in nurse uniform, performs fellatio on him mid-operation... **LSD** is a film which grows more and more ridiculous the longer it progresses, culminating in the doctor chasing Yoko around wearing a gore-soaked cardboard box. It finally fails to convince either as a trip or as a nightmare and has next to no cinematic value, but just about makes it as some kind of hybrid splatterpunk/Noh performance piece – which, even then, can barely sustain repeat viewing.

Of a similar nature to the first two **Guinea Pig** films is the **All Night Long** trilogy of films by Katsuya Matsumura, which commenced in 1992 with **All Night Long,** continued with **Atrocity** (1994), and finished with **Final Atrocity** (1996). All three of these bleak, nihilistic films are concerned with the meaningless of human existence and the subsequent worthlessness of human life, expressed in terms of sadistic torture and murder but also by verbal philosophy. Like **Guinea Pig**, they take sadism beyond the merely sexual into the *truly* Sadean realm of the homicidal, but in doing so never discriminate in favour of either gender – both male and female victims are abused and dispatched with equal dispassion, and only the strongest survive. Matsumura chooses the world of highschool students in which to play out his dangerous ideas, pitting groups of youths against each other in fatal opposition and observing how exposure to violence ultimately induces even greater violence in those born to be "winners", while the weaker succumb to the death instinct. In **All Night Long**, three teenagers are baptised in bloody murder when they witness a backstreet killing; the latent instincts aroused by this corruption lead them to further abuse a female friend who has been raped, before they trap and slay the rapist. But the next film, **Atrocity**, takes Matsumura's controversial ethos to a far greater extreme – so much so that it was refused a certificate by Eirin for its "unacceptable tone", and finally released straight to video.

The protagonist of **Atrocity** is Shinichi, a bespectacled weakling into computers and dolls, who in the school holidays finds himself being persecuted by a gang of violent delinquents. The gang's (nameless) leader is a rich young psychopathic homosexual, who surrounds himself with explicit anatomical drawings and holocaust photographs and whose penchant for dissociated violence is illustrated by such acts as ripping apart a live hamster and filling one of his boyfriend's ears with superglue. He carries a cylindrical blowtorch and punctuates his every act of inhuman cruelty with a whispered "I'm sorry". An effete conflation of Nietzsche, de Sade and Ilsa Koch, his character is summed up by his adoption of James Dean's legendary philosophy: "live fast, die young, and leave a good-looking corpse".

At the start of **Atrocity**, Shinichi is beaten up by the gang, stripped naked and has a lit cigarette stubbed out on his genitals. The next day he is visited by the psycho alone, who drives him to his well-appointed countryside house. Here he is introduced to a female slave, a pathetic creature who has been hooked on heroin, gang-raped and tortured (her fingernails pulled out one by one) into total submission. Shinichi is forced to watch as the psycho humiliates the girl, feeding her like a dog and making her dance naked before beating her so badly with a poker that she pisses all over the floor. It is during this sequence that we see the first stirrings of a darker nature in Shinichi, who kicks her when she absent-mindedly laughs at him. The girl is finally dumped in a garbage bin and doused with alcohol, and only Shinichi's pleading intervention prevents her from being torched alive. At this point the relationship between Shinichi and the psycho is ambivalent; the psycho constantly tries to seduce Shinichi, and declares no interest in the actions of his gang, whom he describes as "freaks"; yet he avows that he and Shinichi can never be friends, and latent violence toward the unfortunate youth is never far beneath the surface.

Next day Shinichi meets two new friends through the Internet and asks them back to his house (his parents are on vacation). One of these boys asks his girlfriend, Sayaka, to come over. When the psycho and his gang pay an unexpected visit, Shinichi and his guests are tied up and kidnapped, taken back to the countryside house to play a "game" – a game which can only result in massacre. Sayaka is stripped nude and shot up with heroin while her boyfriend is forced to watch; his companion's face is horribly cut up with a switchblade; and Shinichi's chest is hideously burned by the psycho's blowtorch when he rejects the latter's sexual advances. But later, when the psycho is throttling Sayaka in the bath, Shinichi once more gains an insight into the potential rewards of sadism and violence.

The psycho selects the comatose Sayaka as next victim; her boyfriend must slowly slice her apart with a bayonet, bit by bit, until she dies. If he does not cut deeply enough, his skull will be smashed by the baseball bat-wielding thug who stands poised behind him. At the last minute the boy turns and bayonets the thug in the stomach, snatches up the fallen bat and knocks the psycho senseless, then smashes another gang member's skull to pulp. As the remaining thug advances with menacing switchblade, he trips over Sayaka and Shinichi runs him through with the bayonet. He then savagely finishes off the other stabbed gang member, plunging the blade into his genitals and twisting. Finally, Shinichi is ready to take his revenge on the psycho, whom he ties in a chair before sprinkling his face with gasoline. Wielding the psycho's own blowtorch, he applies the flame to his captive's face until the smoking flesh is cooked and the psycho dies in screaming agony. "I'm sorry."

Shinichi is now revelling in violence and slaughter. He locates the last two survivors, Sayaka and her boyfriend, and butchers them as they make love. He stands laughing and gloating over the bodies, joyous at the "meaningless" murders, before quitting the house and going home to prepare for school the next day. "This happiness can only be understood by certain people."

Final Atrocity is a reprise of its predecessor, again charting the progress of a highschool student from shy introvert to psychopathic killer, and relentless in its assertion that human beings are as insignificant as insects. Like **Guinea Pig** – though more eloquent in exposition – the **All Night Long** films are not merely mindless exploitation but deliberated, convincing Sadean essays in nihilism, the assertion of will over others, and the void at the heart of modern society which can and does foment potentially genocidal alienation.

While the Japanese excel at this kind of realistic violence, their more conventional, "fantastic" horror movies – such as **Nighty Night, Tastiest Flesh, Cyclops** or the much-praised **Evil Dead Trap** series – are mostly disappointing, particularly in the light of the contemporaneous strand of cyber-carnage cinema epitomised by Shinya Tsukamoto's innovative **Tetsuo** (1990)[6]. The first **Evil Dead Trap** (Toshiharu Ikeda's **Shiryo No Wana**, 1988), for example, is ultimately little more than a formulaic slasher movie – albeit with Argentoesque pretensions and occasionally interesting camera effects – with a cop-out supernatural[7] ending. The film starts promisingly – a female TV reporter is sent a videotape which turns out to be a snuff movie. This film within a film, briefly glimpsed, contains what must be the most graphic, realistic and unpleasant eyeball-piercing beyond **Guinea Pig,** as the female victim's eye is punctured by a blade and its viscous contents drool forth. But from that point on, when the girl and four friends decide – somewhat unwisely – to investigate the deserted factory complex where the snuff movie was shot, **Evil Dead Trap** descends into a series of slasher clichés culminating in a hackneyed stomach-bursting demon baby scenario. There is hardly any sex, just a brief coupling and a rape which mostly occurs off-screen, and very little torture; the girls are killed relatively cleanly, and this is far from being cutting-edge

*Toshiharu Ikeda's **Evil Dead Trap***

Japanese sex and violence. Izo Hashimoto's **Shiryo No Wana 2: Hideki (Evil Dead Trap 2: Hideki,** 1991) and Toshiharu Ikeda's **Shiryo No Wana 3: Chigireta No Satsujin (Evil Dead Trap 3: Broken Love Killer,** 1993) duly followed.

By far the best of the contemporary "horror" movies is Kazuo Komizu's[8] XXX Nikkatsu production **Shojo No Harawata (Entrails Of A Virgin,** 1988), in fact an unrelenting sex film set in a generic horror milieu, which largely avoids the derivative manipulations of its closest peers in defining an oneiric zone where sex and violent death are interchangeable.

This downbeat, desolated film opens with a group of three girls and three young men on a mountain photo shoot. These scenes are intercut with extended soft porn sequences of various group members engaged in sex acts; these inserts are, presumably, the fantasies of the three males. As night falls they drive back to a lodge, the fantasy sections continuing but now intermingled with intimations of vague evil. The road is swathed in fog; we glimpse a naked figure, coated in mud, rising up as if from a leafy ditch by the roadside.

Back at the lodge, the group eat dinner and begin to engage in suggestive play. Boy One and Girl One strip to their underwear and Boy One torments her with various wrestling holds, until in a close-up crotch-shot she pisses in her white panties, then passes out. The mysterious, mud-caked figure lurks outside in the shadows. Boy One ventures out to the car, and is suddenly confronted by the stranger who is wielding a hammer. As the pair face each other – the stranger appearing to be of huge stature – seconds of silence pass. From this stasis the screen suddenly flashes into a strobic concatenation of freefall pre-death images, then the hammer-blow is delivered and utterly caves in Boy One's skull, his eyeballs bursting from their ruined sockets and slithering over plates of shattered bone.

Meanwhile, the other four (Girl One remains unconscious) pair off; Boy

Two and Girl Two come to grips on the floor, while Boy Three and Girl Three abscond to the the garden. Both couples engage in extended foreplay; Boy Three, drunk on bourbon, bites Girl Three on the nipple, she runs off but he catches up with her and as he lifts her upside-down they perform 69 in a standing position. Afterwards she slumps to the floor, spitting out a copious flood of semen and then, apparently perturbed, wanders off into the garden. A great phallic shadow falls across her, then she is lifted up onto the balcony and violently fucked by the stranger, whose member is shown to be a massive, equine organ. As she sprawls forward in the aftermath, a lantern above her fragments; a sheet of jagged glass drops down and, like a vitreous guillotine blade, decapitates her. Boy Three, staggering around in search of the girl, is confronted by the stranger who now wields a long iron spike. Again we see a string of flashing images, then Boy Three is transfixed by the spike which enters at his shoulder and exits pinning him to the ground, dead where he stands.

Back inside, Boy Two and Girl Two are fucking. They are interrupted by the topless Girl One, who has revived but appears detached, somnambulistic. She wanders outside and appears sexually demented, rubbing her crotch against a tree-trunk, then finding Girl Three's head whose bloody mouth she tongues and kisses ecstatically. Returning to the lodge she finds Boy Two and Girl Two fucking in a cupboard, tosses the severed head at them. Boy Two flees outside and is soon strung up with a meathook through his throat. Girl One, now completely nude, acts with increasing sexual frenzy, performing fellatio on the dead Boy Three then fingering herself as she writhes on the ground. The stranger appears, rips off the corpse's arm and throws it to her like a bone to a rabid dog. She begins to masturbate with the severed limb, its stiff fingers raking her vulva. As the stranger approaches she starts to suck his huge, pulsating erection, then he impales her with it, finally shooting thick rivers of cum over her chest and face. Then follows probably the most bizarre fistfuck on film, as the stranger inserts his hand to the elbow, stretching the skin of her belly as he rummages inside, before withdrawing with a handful of her bloody innards.

Girl Two, hysterical, is now the sole survivor. She seeks refuge in an outhouse but the murderous, priapic stranger tracks her down and rapes her. We see them copulating in various positions, before an unprecedented cum-shot: his seed, blossoming in thick white clouds into the raw red lining of her vulva, viewed from *inside* her body. After this, the stranger disappears as suddenly, as mysteriously as he had appeared. Cut to Girl Two, heavily pregnant, pensive atop a bleak hilltop. Rocks ignite in burst of fire; freezeframe. The end credits are followed by a brief shot of a foetus. Fade to black.

Entrails Of A Virgin at times approximates a live-action erotic *anime*, but at the death supplants comic-strip sensibilities with a more sombre, chilling and remorseless vision. Perhaps the first true "pink horror" film, **Entrails Of A Virgin** is a bleak, muted document of sexual hysteria with hallucinatory montages – an orgasmic nightmare. It is a film which lures the casual viewer with comforting genre accoutrements and *mise-en-scène*[9], but ultimately conveys only the horrific futility of the sexual impulse.

All pretensions of plot are forgotten in films which in different ways perhaps represent the terminal exposition of female death: the *hara kiri* videos of Masami Akita[10], and the mondo/snuff documentary series **Death Women**.

Masami Akita's **Lost Paradise** (Right Brain Productions, 1990) is typical of his work. With a soundtrack by the director himself, this intense and vivid film shows a young woman taking her own life by an act of ritual *hara kiri*.[11] Dressed in militaristic attire, the girl (Asako Mochuzuki) kneels, removes her jacket and opens her shirt to the waist, exposing her naked breasts and stomach. Lowering the waistband of her white panties, she caresses her belly before taking up a sacrificial knife, whose blade she wraps in a white bandage. Pressing the point into her left side she punctures the flesh, then slowly and deliberately pulls the knife across to the right. First blood leaks out, then as the gash widens her entrails start to ooze onto the floor. She continues the cut, her moans strongly reminiscent of those made by the actresses in porno films. Finally she collapses, still groaning, in a lake of blood and coiling viscera. Her death throes are extremely protracted. Akita presents this rite of ultimate penetration as an auto-erotic act, the consummation of a death pact pre-ordained by the very sexualization of a woman's flesh. A coda briefly shows the gunshot suicide of an elder man, but the video's *raison d'être* is the girl's "beautiful" death.

In a country where **Faces Of Death** (USA, 1979) reputedly grossed more money than **Star Wars** (USA, 1977), little surprise to find **Death Women**, first in a series of '90s "shockumentary"-style tapes[12] comprising nothing but real-life studies of dead females. Whereas Masami Akita's films present a woman's death as a thing of beauty, **Death Women** is a harsh, often sickening document of the aftermath of fatal violence. The 45 minutes of genuine mondo footage, which appears to originate from Taiwan, are solely concerned with the mutilated, murdered or mangled corpses of females ranging in age from infancy upward. Victims of homicidal rape, drowning, gunshot murder/suicide, earthquake, incineration, stabbing, traffic accidents, plane crashes and other fatal traumas are examined in unflinching detail. Among the "highlights" of the film are a recently stabbed woman's body leaking dark beads of blood, a woman pulverised by a bus literally falling to pieces when removed from the wreckage, and a carving knife still jutting from the stomach of a murdered child. An abortion is also shown, the red liquidised flesh of a (female?) embryo sucked into a glass tube. The

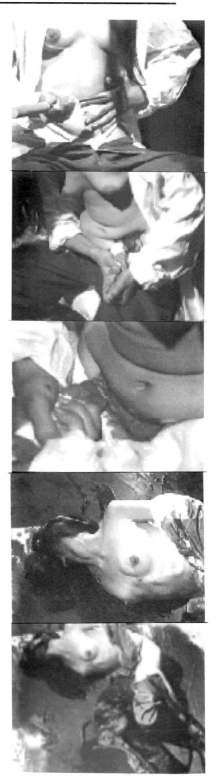

Masami Akita's **Lost Paradise**

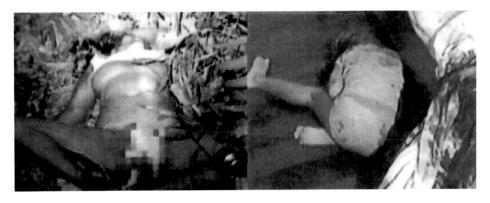

Death Women

episodes are linked by footage from a particularly gruesome autopsy, a woman's body deconstructed with indecent disdain.

The film's unknown editors impose a few embellishments; some segments are solarized, maudlin piano motifs underscore scenes of dead children, white borders occasionally alter the screen shape focusing attention on areas of physical demolition. Typically, digital masking censors the genitals of some corpses, although their severed heads, spilt brains or guts are lovingly lensed, a woman's face even turned to give the best possible profile[13]. And in a twist which combines this element of censorship with distinctly pornographic resonances, the female corpse which is being butchered under autopsy remains demurely dressed in spotless white panties, suggesting a necrophiliac fetishism only viable at the end-zone of cultural extremes.

At least eight volumes of **Death Women** have been issued to date.

NOTES

1 • Hideshi Hino was born in Manchuria, 1946. His debut *manga* strip, *Tsumetai Ase* (*Cold Sweat*) appeared in 1967, and was introduced in Osamu Tezuka's experimental magazine *COM*. Hino went on to produce a series of grotesque strips featuring freaks, psycho-killers and other deviants, which appeared in magazines such as *Shonen Gaho* and Katsuichi Magai's iconoclastic *Garo*. His reputation as a master of the grotesque soon became firmly established, and alongside Suehiro Maruo he remains a key exponent of the "atrocity" style. Hino is best known in the West for his infernal *manga* holocaust *Jigoku-hen* (*Panorama Of Hell*, 1982), and *Kyofu Zigoku-shojo* (*Hell Baby*, 1989), both published in English by Blast Books of New York. In the absence of an acknowledged director for **Guinea Pig 1**, it has been speculated that Hino is also responsible for this video – although this seems quite unlikely.

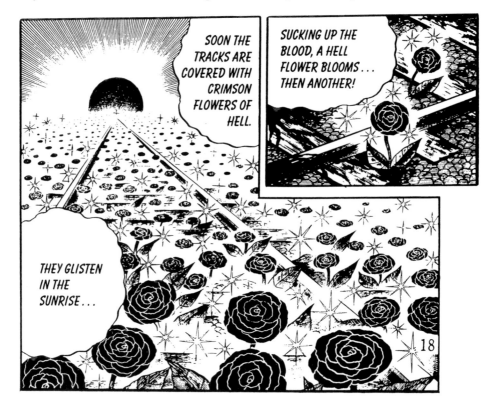

Hideshi Hino's "Panorama Of Hell" (© *Blast Books*)

2 • Indeed, the SFX in **Guinea Pig 2** are so convincing that Hollywood moron Charlie Sheen, upon watching a copy of the film, decided he had stumbled onto a genuine snuff movie, even going so far as alerting the FBI to his shocking "discovery".

3 • A full account and critique of **Guinea Pig 2** appears on pages 173–175 of the definitive death movie study *Killing For Culture* by David Kerekes and David Slater (Creation Books, 1995); the following extract describes some of the film's murderous action:

> "*After caressing her thigh for a moment, the Samurai administers a drug to the girl and picks up a pair of shears, clacking them loudly. He then cuts through the victim's clothing. The scene fades upon him reaching her underwear. When the scene returns, a white sheet covers the victim. The Samurai raises a bradawl and plunges it*

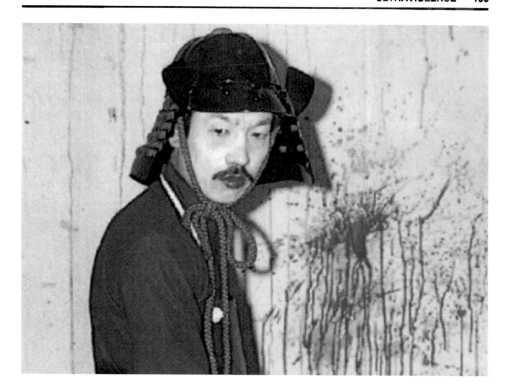

Guinea Pig 2

into the girl (it isn't clear whereabouts: penetration of flesh is depicted in extreme close-up; reaction shots follow). He mumbles to himself before commencing to slice off her left hand. Again, as with each subsequent mutilation shot, the deed is performed in isolated close-up, with intermittent edits to the face of the Samurai and the victim, dazed and delirious. Blood spatters as the killer struggles to break the hand away at the wrist. It is an effective sequence, but not wholly convincing. He slices off the other hand, then commences on the arms. When gristle proves a problem, he takes a hammer and chisel to ease removal. Again, despite it being effective, the whole attitude of the arm hacking seems wrong. A heartbeat wells up on the soundtrack. With both hands and arms removed (the film doesn't show the second arm amputation), the Samurai turns his attention to the lower extremities. He saws off one leg, lifts it to his face and caresses it longingly. The film doesn't reveal the removal of the other leg, but shoots straight into the next sequence. Drawing the sheet up the limbless, still living body, the camera avoids the genital area by focusing upon the victim's navel (her breasts remain covered by the sheet). The Samurai incises the torso with a scalpel. A synthesised orchestration accompanies. As he prods his hands into the wound, a cutaway reveals a red trickle running down from the girl's mouth. When he thrusts his hands deep inside the wound, the girl vomits a mouthful of blood. Her head rolls sidewards and she dies. The Samurai pulls from the abdomen a handful of intestines and organs. He raises a machete and, in slow motion, hacks off her head. It flips through the air and comes to rest on the floor. The Samurai props it up on the bed and enucleates an eyeball with a dinner spoon. He sucks on it, cross-eyed with delight. Finally, in a clichéd, post-coitus gesture, the Samurai smokes a cigarette."

4 • The evisceration of a woman as ritual relates to *hara kiri*, an ancient act in which female votives would offer up the "flower" of their entrails and blood by a self-inflicted knife wound, a version of *seppuku* marked by religious ecstasy – a state apparently induced in **Flower Of Bloody Flesh** by the administering of drugs [see also note 11].

5 • The first two **Guinea Pig** films are Midnight 25 Video releases. Subsequent releases in the series, on Japan Home Video, are milder and more glossy fantasy-orientated entries such as the inane **Android Of Notre Dame** (1989, also somewhat confusingly labelled "**Guinea Pig 2**") and the slightly more coherent **Guinea Pig 4: Mermaid In A Manhole** (1991, also directed by Hideshi Hino). This change in direction was possibly occasioned by public reaction to the first two movies, amid growing speculation that one or both were genuine snuff films.

Hideshi Hino's **Mermaid In A Manhole**

6 • While the utter destruction of the flesh is paramount in films like **Guinea Pig 2** and **Atrocity**, its mutability seems to offer an equally nightmarish future in the cycle of underground/cyberpunk cinema which includes Shinya Tsukamoto's **Tetsuo**, Shigeru Izumiya's **Death Powder** (1987), and Shojin Fukui's **Pinocchio 964** (1992) and **Rubber's Lover** (1996) [see chapter 8].

Shinya Tsukamoto's **Tetsuo**

If this trope of physical mutation can be attributed to the ghosts of Hiroshima, then in terms of Japanese SF cinema it traces back to the '50s films of Inoshiro Honda, most famous for Toho *kaiju eiga* ("monster movies") such as **Godzilla** (1954, in which a giant prehistoric reptile is awoken by an Atomic blast), **Rodan** (1956, a pterodactyl), **Varan** (1958), **Mothra** (1961, a giant she-moth), and **Ghidrah** (1965, a three-headed dragon). The **Godzilla** series has persisted to this day, its global popularity culminating in the high-tech 1998 Hollywood version. Besides these world-famous onslaughts of acid bubblegum reptilia, Honda also produced a pair of notably trippy, downbeat works in **Bijo To Ekitai Ningen (H-Man**, 1958) and **Matango (Attack Of The Mushroom People**, 1963). In **H-Man**, a drug-dealer is exposed to nuclear radiation and contaminates everybody he touches, turning them to radioactive fluid. **Matango** evokes the Atomic fall-out cloud even more directly, as islanders addicted to a psychedelic fungus start to mutate, turning into half-human, half-mushroom creatures. Both films resonate with post-Atomic angst, the screen awash with heavy liquid visions which fuel the pulp plotlines.

Inoshiro Honda's **Matango**

While the pessimism of **H-Man** and **Matango** is recalled in occasional films such as Hajime Sato's **Kyuketsuki Gokemidoro (Goke, Bodysnatcher From Hell**, 1968) – the Earth is over-run by blood-sucking, skull-fucking parasites – most '60s Japanese SF strays toward the kiddie-oriented *kaiju eiga*, which peaked in 1968 with Honda's **Kaiju Soshingeki (Destroy All Monsters)**, or "superhero" fare such as the **Ultraman** series. At the most sublime end of the scale, however, are the symbolistic collaborations between the writer Kobo Abe and director Hiroshi Teshigahara, such as **Otoshi Ana (Pitfall**, 1962) and **Moetsukita Chizu (The Ruined Map**, 1968). Abe, whose novels feature Ballardian notions of identity implosion and the zoning of inner space to postulate the human body/psyche itself as ultimate event horizon, also wrote the screenplays for Teshigahara's film adaptations. Best known in the West is **Suna No Onna (Woman Of The Dunes**, 1964), an exercise in claustrophobic eroticism in which extreme close-ups

Hiroshi Teshigahara's Face Of Another

make a woman's skin resemble the lunar surface, but the most intriguing is **Tanin No Kao (The Face Of Another**, 1967). A hideously burned man disguises his face in flesh-like plastic in order to make love to his wife in the guise of another; at the same time, a girl terribly burnt at Hiroshima kills herself after allowing her brother to caress her scars and seduce her. Teshigahara conjures palpable alienation and abjection from a warped, clinical *milieu*.

7 • The literal translation of **Shiryo No Wana** is in fact "trap of the dead ghost", and ghost stories have long comprised the main strand of Japanese horror cinema. Outstanding early examples include Kenji Mizoguchi's **Ugetsu Monogatari (Tales Of The Pale Moon After Rain**, 1953); Nobuo Nakagawa's **Kaidan Kasane-ga-fuchi (Ghost Story Of Kasane Swamp**, 1959), **Tokaido Yotsuya Kaidan (Ghost Story Of Yotsuya**, 1959) and **Jigoku (Hell**, 1960); and Masaki Kobayashi's **Kwaidan** (1964). **Kwaidan**, one of the best-known of all Japanese films in the West, consists of four episodes based on ghost stories by Lafcadio Hearn. In *Kurokami* ("The Black Hair") a samurai beds his wife only to find her a rotting corpse by morning; in *Yuki-Onna* ("The Snow Woman") a beautiful spectre lures men to a frozen death; in *Miminashi Hoichi No Hanashi* ("Hoichi The Earless") a musician is painted with runes to ward off ghosts, but his ears, left uncovered, are ripped off; and in *Chawan No Naka* ("In A Cup Of Tea") a samurai sees a ghost's face in a teacup. Produced in accordance with Western viewing dictates, **Kwaidan** was a failure in Japan.

Hajime Sato's **Kaidan Semushi Otoko (Ghost Of The Hunchback**, 1965) and Tsuneo Kobayashi's **Kaidan Katame No Otoko (Ghost Of The One-Eyed Man**, 1965) are notable for their stylistic emulation of Italian directors such as Mario Bava, Riccardo Freda and Antonio Margheriti. Kaneto Shindo's **Yabu No Naka Kuroneko (Kuroneko**, 1968) is a reprise of sorts of his earlier **Onibaba** [see chapter 3], a *bakeneko mono* ("cat ghost story") concerning a woman and her daughter-in-law, who are raped and

Masaki Kobayashi's **Kwaidan**

Kaneto Shindo's **Kuroneko**

murdered by a samurai. They return as ghost cats, sworn to kill all samurai. The warrior sent to dispatch them turns out to be the son of one, husband of the other, resulting in a bizarre climax.

Other *bakeneko mono* films include Yoshihiro Ishikawa's **Kaibyo Noroi Numa (Ghost Cat Of The Haunted Swamp**, 1968); Tokizo Tanaka's **Hiroku Kaibyoden (The Haunted Castle**, 1969); and Teruo Ishii's **Kaidan Nobori Ryu (Blind Woman's Curse**, 1970). Another exploitative strain of ghost films are those based more in a specifically erotic milieu, including such low-grade entries as Baku Komori's **Jain (Snake Lust**, 1967) and Giichi Nishihara's **Sei No Kaidan (Ghost Story Of Sex**, 1972); Nagisa Oshima's **Empire Of Passion** is probably the most respectable variation.

Of other stand-out supernatural films, Kimiyoshi Yasuda's **Yokai Hyaku Monogatari (One Hundred Monsters**, 1968) features a variety of misshapen phantoms laying waste to a brothel; Shiro Toyoda's **Jigokuhen (Hell Screen**, 1969) tells the story of an artist prepared to sacrifice his daughter's life in pursuit of achieving the perfect painting; Masahiro Shinoda's **Sakura No Mori No Mankai No Shita (Under The Cherry Blossoms**, 1975) is a bloody but beautiful tale of a haunted cherry-blossom grove; Nobuhiko Obayashi's **Ie (House**, 1977) is the vivid tale of a house which, possessed by a sexually frustrated spirit, comes alive and devours young virgins; former pink film director Tatsumi Kumashiro's re-make of **Jigoku (Inferno**, 1981) depicts Hell as a psychedelic labyrinth of pain in which sinners are dismembered, broken on burning wheels, and even eaten, by hideous demons for all eternity; and Kiyoshi Kurosawa's **Sweet Home** (1989), with SFX by Dick Smith, is perhaps the ultimate haunted house movie. While all these movies have inspired moments, in general they fall short of the frenetic, non-stop pulp excess supplied by the very best Hong Kong horrors such as Ho Menga's **Black Magic 2** (1981) or Yang Chuan's **Seeding Of A Ghost** (1986).

8 • Komizu, who usually signatures his films with the cinenym "Gaira", is a former protégé of Koji Wakamatsu, and a pink/pulp director of some renown whose other movies have included **Bijo No Harawata (Entrails Of A Beauty**, 1986), **Gomon Kifujin (Female Inquisitor**, 1987), **Batoru Garu (Battle Girl** *aka* **The Living Dead In Tokyo Bay**, 1992) and **XX: Utsukushiki Hyoteki (XX: Beautiful Weapon**, 1993). He also acted as cameraman on Shigeru Izumiya's cyberpunk experiment **Death Powder** [see chapter 8].

9 • Like the "haunted" house in Robert Wise's **The Haunting**, the psycho-killer-rapist of **Entrails Of A Virgin** owes his apparently supernatural characteristics to the libidinal hysteria of the victims; therefore, though in superficial terms the film could be compared to "slasher" films like John Carpenter's **Halloween** or "demonic possession" films like Sam Raimi's **Evil Dead**, Kazuo merely manipulates these pulp formats to investigate a claustrophobic sex/death collision clearly intelligible as Sadean. **Entrails Of A Virgin** is a tract on fatal sexual dementia whose closest peers in Western cinema are probably, in fact, films by Walerian Borowczyk such as **The Beast** and, in particular, **Blood Of Dr Jekyll**.

10 • Masami Akita is also one of Japan's leading underground noise musicians, performing and recording under the name Merzbow. Ian Kerkhof's documentary **Beyond Ultra Violence – Uneasy Listening By Merzbow** (1997, NL) is a fragmentary but compelling account of Akita's music (described as "demonic electronic assaults from the universal god of noise"), his philosophy and influences.

11 • *Hara kiri* differs from *seppuku* in that there is no decapitation following the disembowelling. *Hara kiri* is not actually regarded as an act of suicide, rather it is a positive act of religious beauty, traditionally an offering of the female's entrails to the gods. This erotic film treatment of female suicide can also be found in pink movies such as Norifumi Suzuki's **The Sex-Crazed Daimyo**, although Akita appears to be alone in dedicating entire films to the subject. With rope-master Chimuo Nureki, Akita conceived the notion for a series of Kinbiken videos (called the Right Brain series) on the theme of *hara kiri*, presented ritualistically in the same way as their *kinbaku* collaborations [see chapter 3]. The fetishistic links between *hara kiri*, military uniforms and S/M practices are also to be found in **Shitsuraku-en**, a video based on the writings of Hideo Fujiyama and produced by *Kitan Club*, Japan's leading fetish magazine.

Kentaro Uchida's **The Shocks**

12 • Other Japanese shockumentaries have ranged from Nobuo Nakagawa's **Spots In The Sun** (1964) to Kentaro Uchida's **The Shocks** (1987), which generated several sequels, and the more recent **Death Files** series. These bloody, disturbing movies – which border on "snuff" – are big, mainstream box-office in Japan. In *Killing For Culture*, Kerekes and Slater describe **The Shocks** as follows: *"Scene upon scene of genuine atrocities make it an unrelenting, disconsolate trip into Hell. People leap from burning apartment blocks and cameras follow their lethal fall, right to the nauseating impact on concrete. A daredevil wingwalker is ground into oblivion as the plane on which he stands inverts and gets too close to the runway. The madness prevalent in South Africa manifests with a scapegoat being chased from his home by an enraged mob of neighbours and scoop-seeking cameraman. When caught, the man is stabbed and stoned to death. Another victim is tied to stakes driven in the ground, flattened beneath heavy boulders and finally burned. Assassinations and executions, all horribly real, retain the bleak mood."*

The history of Japanese "mondo" movies can be traced back to Kelzo Ohno's **Nippon No Yoru (Japan By Night, 1962)**; this type of sex documentary continued up and in to the '70s with entries such as Sadao Nakajima's **Nippon 69: Sekkusu Ryoki**

Chitai (Japan 69: Sex Zone, 1969), Sekkusu Dokyumento: Seitosaku No Sekai (Sex Documentary: Student World, 1971), and Poruno No Joo: Nippon Sex Ryoko (Porno Queen: Japanese Sex Trip, 1973).

13 • In 1996, American publishers Feral House published their notorious book *Death Scenes*, a ground-breaking collection of photographs of murder/suicide victims. When the book was imported into Japan, customs officials were reportedly outraged – because a few of the mangled, rotting corpses were *naked*.

GARBAGE MAN

THE WILD WORLD OF TAKAO NAKANO

中野　貴雄

AS well as pink movies, violence, horror, cyberpunk and various underground productions, there is also a strand of uniquely Japanese trash cinema which contains its own fair share of sex, blood and madness. Doyen of the modern trash scene is Takao Nakano who (transvestism aside) might well be described as the Ed Wood of Japanese cinema. Since 1989, Nakano – formerly a promotor of *joshi-puro* (female wrestling) – has produced a catalogue of unashamed trash: no/low-budget movies with titles like **Attack Of Mu-Empire From Deep Sea, Playgirls, Spiral Zone, 54 Nude Honeys, Flower Of Sumo Woman**, and **Mini-Skirt Cops L.E.G.S.**; movies mostly shot on video, which invariably feature frenzied catfights – Nakano's key trademark – between nude or semi-nude girls, plus topless female Sumo wrestlers, sexy karate-kicking secret agent girls, and lashings of gratuitous hardcore sex and cartoon violence, all knowingly played out on the most gaudy, cut-price or plain ridiculous Z-movie sets possible.

Playgirls 2 (1993), for instance, contains one particularly outrageous catfight between two topless, white-pantied girls (one typically tattooed and large-breasted), that involves much bloody wounding including deep biting, flesh-tearing, vaginal mutilation and a chewed-off nipple; the fight ends with the losing girl having a good yard of intestine yanked from her vulva before her left eyeball is smashed out. And in the climactic catfight to **Spiral Zone** (1992), kicks in the crotch are exchanged before the loser is dispatched by a savage bite to the clitoris.

Nakano is perhaps best known outside Japan for his four **Exorsister** films, epics of "tentacle" trash in which the heroine, sweet exorcist Maria Cruel (played by *manga* illustrator Ban Ippongi), fights various sex-mad demons and monsters which are preying on semi-naked schoolgirls, nurses or female office workers. The special effects are cheap, but as convincing as they need be within the crazed logic of Nakano's universe. As well as slime-dripping beasts with priapic tentacles, Nakano fits in his usual quota of sex, bloody mayhem and no-holds-barred catfighting[1].

Exorsister

In 1997 Nakano diversified somewhat by producing two Edo period movies: **Inugami (Legend Of Wolves)**, about an itinerant *ninja* rapist, and **Edo Ohoku Kidan (Secret Life Of Shogun)**, a strange tale of the Shogun's harem. Both retain his penchant for fighting females, merely transposing the action to a previous century.

Takao Nakano is a great student of '60s and '70s Japanese exploitation cinema, and speaks with much enthusiasm about the inspiration he has drawn from this source. He was interviewed by Romain Slocombe in Tokyo, April 1997.

ROMAIN SLOCOMBE: Since when have you been interested in films?
TAKAO NAKANO: I've been interested in films since I was 15. In Japan, we have public baths called *taishuyokujo*. I used to go to the public baths with my mum and dad, and there I saw all kinds of posters for films showing at the cinemas nearby at that time. Among them, there were posters for porn films, monster films and many other kinds of films. Having seen these posters, I secretly wished to see the porn films, even at the age of 9 or 10. But I wasn't allowed to see such X-rated films, or "bizarre" films, because I was too young. When I was 15, I somehow began to be able to go to the porn cinema by hiding the fact that I was a junior high school student, only a boy, and pretending to be an adult by wearing my dad's coat. I must have looked so strange wearing a thick coat in summer. During my childhood, that's when I began to have an interest in films.
RS: Isn't it illegal to put up porn film posters in public places?
TN: Yes, but in the past, when I was a child, which is more than 20 years ago now, regulation wasn't that strict. It was OK to put up porn film posters in public

Secret Life Of Shogun (© Romain Slocombe)

places. Putting up such posters around schools might have been prohibited but the matter was practically left to take its own course. So we could see them everywhere. But I wasn't allowed to see porn films because I was too young. So I tried hard to imagine what these films were like. And now, though I wanna see the films which I couldn't at that time, it's not possible because they've been scrapped. One of those scrapped films which I wanted to see as a child is a motorbiker film. There used to be woman motorbiker films, or *onna bosozoku* films. It's been so frustrating that I can't see them, even though I've reached the age when I'm allowed to see such X-rated films, that now I incorporate the concept of these scrapped films into my own films as a kind of revenge.

RS: I suppose many aspects of Japanese culture can be rather grotesque or shocking.

TN: I think one of the reasons for that is what the Japanese perceive as grotesque and what Western people perceive as grotesque is different. What the Japanese didn't mean to create as particularly grotesque or bizarre could be perceived as completely the opposite by Western people. For example, the film called **Kozure Ookami**, or **Shogun Assassin**, was actually made to be very serious[2]. Its brutal scenes marked by spurting blood were made not to titillate the audience, but to earnestly entertain them.

RS: There is no regulation of violent scenes in Japan, is there?

TN: No, but the murder case of Miyazaki [see chapter 5, note 3] has recently been headline news, and since then people have begun to frown at violent scenes.

They're practically being overlooked though. There's been a movement trying to regulate violent scenes but it's always been ineffectual. So, in Japan, apart from "mosaics" [digital censorship] which are regulated by the government, I think there're almost no ethics in making films. In short, anything could be shown as long as the parts between the legs are hidden.

RS: There's the word *ero-guro* in Japanese. What does it mean?

TN: It used to be called *eroguronansensu*. It means eroticism, grotesqueness, and nonsense. There was the era called Taisho [1912–26], that's the age of the Taisho Emperor before the Showa Emperor which lasted for more than 60 years, and *eroguronansensu* was popular in the Taisho era. Then Japan rushed into the Second World War, but the word *eroguronansensu* had come into fashion before that. So, Japan's democracy and *eroguronansensu* are actually a set; they happened at about the same time. In short, *ero-guro* is a word, a sort of key word, for the combined concepts of eroticism and grotesqueness.

RS: Are there any particular directors who have the concept of *ero-guro* in their films?

TN: Well, I'd say Teruo Ishii and Kenji Misumi, though he might be offended by being categorised as an *ero-guro* director[3]. Our company is called Raizoh, which was named after the samurai actor Raizoh Ichikawa[4]. He played in the series called **Kyoshiro Nemuri [Son Of Black Mass]**, which are indeed samurai films with a mixture of eroticism, a kind of grotesqueness, and hard-boiledness.

RS: Kyoshiro Nemuri is a sort of anti-hero, isn't he?

TN: Yes. He's a mixed blood (only half Japanese). There was an unfortunate period 500 years ago when Christian missionaries were suppressed in Japan[5], and Kyoshiro Nemuri may be a hard-boiled hero created from a mixture of many things including the memory of the suppression of Christianity.

RS: He kills people, doesn't he?

TN: He does. He kills both good and bad people, men and women.

RS: It may be accepted because he's a mixed blood. Are there any other negative heroes?

TN: In Japan, from the Taisho era to the beginning of the Showa era, between 1920 and 1930, hero series like **Daibosatsu-toge [Great Bodhisattva Pass]**[6], in which a blind man called Ryunosuke Tsukue travels, cutting people with his sword, were popular. Nihilism and nihilists were just in fashion at that time and **Kyoshiro Nemuri** was actually derived from the concepts of nihilistic heroes. It was in the second half of the 1960s that spurting blood began to be seen on screens in Japan. Before that, films in which we could see people cut with swords, splashing blood, and naked women hadn't existed, though their concept had been like that.

RS: Did you go to the cinema to see these films when they were on?

TN: No, I wasn't allowed because I was too young. So, I tried hard to imagine that these films might have been like this or like that.

RS: Since when and by whom have you been influenced?

TN: When I was 20, which is 15 or 16 years ago now, there was a sort of fad of seeing these films, and I saw the films of Teruo Ishii and Kenji Misumi. Also, there was a period called the "Baburu [Bubble] economy". During the Baburu economy, which is 5, 6 years ago now, or even more, 10 years ago, a video boom happened and almost every family bought a VHS video machine. It was a period when we could see all kinds of films. We could see films like A.C. Stevens' **Orgy Of The Dead** [USA, 1965] and Ed Wood's **Plan Nine From Outer Space** [USA, 1959]. At that time, even some rubbish films like Philippine action movies and Mexican vampire films were bought by Japanese video companies, who distributed them as rental videos. Following this boom, I saw a lot of films.

RS: Then gradually you began to make your own films?

TN: Yes.

RS: How did it go?

TN: Thanks to the video boom, I could see the "bizarre" films I'd wanted to when I was a child, but I always found them not that great. From the point of view of our own existing standard, or ethics, they're not something special. I felt disappointed and let down. Perhaps I shouldn't have seen these old films. I should have let them grow only in my imagination and kept them in my heart.

RS: How did you get the opportunity to actually make a film?

TN: That was not incredible but simple; I made the opportunity simply by working hard. There are many senior directors in film circles. I worked under them, being scolded and saying "I'm sorry, I'm sorry," and then, gradually, opportunities increased where I could speak my opinions. I created conditions in which I could make my own videos by sometimes flattering one person then another person, doing something not interesting at all. It wasn't like I got money and produced films by myself. I didn't have such an experience. Always, some video company provided money for me and I made a film within the limits of that budget.

RS: Who are those senior directors?

TN: I'm now in the industry of pink films; pink films are what we call porn films. There are directors called "Pink Shitenno" ["Pink Best 4"], who've succeeded in the pink film industry. The senior directors under whom I worked when entering the industry include the Pink Shitenno. I don't think you know them, even if I told you their names here.

RS: Go on.

TN: Toshiki Satoh, Hisayasu Sato, Takahisa Zeze, and Kazuhiro Sano. Recently, there's a movement called "Pink New Wave", and within this movement, they've been invited to show their films by Athènes France, which is a sort of association, or maybe a school, organised by France and Japan. This generation of senior directors is rather art-oriented.

RS: Is Gaira one of them?

TN: Gaira belongs to a slightly older generation. He's in his 50s, isn't he? It was Gaira under whom I trained for pink films when I came to Tokyo for the first time. He's been making pink films since the end of the 1960s; he was working under a great director called Koji Wakamatsu.

RS: Have you worked with Gaira?

TN: Twice, making pink films.

RS: Since when have you been working as a director yourself?

TN: Since 1989. I became a director 8 years ago.

RS: How many works have you made since then?

RS: The works I've directed are about 30, I believe. Between 20 and 30. I don't know the precise number because I've never counted them.

RS: Are they mainly videos?

TN: Yes, they are. Two of them are cinema films; one is an omnibus film directed by a couple of people, including myself, and the other is my own film named **Spiral Zone**, and the rest are all videos.

RS: Congratulations on **Spiral Zone** winning a prize.[7]

TN: Oh, thank you.

RS: I suppose you've already started a new film?

Playgirls 2

TN: Well, it's been rather difficult. At the moment, my new film is still at the planning stage and it'll be some time before I actually start shooting it.
RS: Can you present your preferred ideas freely in your videos?
TN: It would be ideal if I could do only what I like, but it's only an ideal and usually there's an outline which I have to follow, in other words, a concept or a theme for a product. I think my ideas may be presented through the method I follow. For example, in casting. It would be ideal if I could cast a girl of my type, but nowadays, people who invest in films wish to maintain a controlling interest. Working with such commercialism, I don't think it's possible to do strictly only what I like.
RS: If you could cast actresses as you like, which kind of actresses would you choose?
TN: It's got to be a girl with big tits. She's also got to be daring with slanted eyes. I love a typical Asian face. A girl who has a face like a fox, big tits, and a tight waist – the topic is changing into my taste in women, isn't it? I would choose such a bold, quarrelsome and hot-blooded girl.
RS: Is that why you're interested in cat fights?
TN: Yes, in a way. I like those kind of girls. Male actors are actually not so important. If we can get along, that's fine. If they're good friends, that's enough for us. Actresses don't need to be our friends.
RS: In **Spiral Zone**, a lot of people look parodic of Japanese culture. They mean something for Japanese people, don't they? The Emperor appears in the film, for example.
TN: That's right; I can't talk out loud about it though. Some films in the 1950s or

Flower Of Sumo Woman (© *Romain Slocombe*)

the 1960s were like that, I mean, boisterous, knockabout. Nowadays, such boisterous knockabout culture has moved to TV. People make slapstick only for TV. There used to be slapstick films but, now, Japanese film makers can't make them.

RS: I think Seijun Suzuki's *yakuza* films such as **Tokyo Nagaremono [Tokyo Drifter]** are the same kind of parody.[8]

TN: That film includes many artistic experiments. All of a sudden, the background turns into red, yellow or blue, for example. Because of this, he wasn't allowed to make any more films at the production company, Nikkatsu.

RS: For example, the hero in **Tokyo Nagaremono** suddenly begins to sing many times, doesn't he – as in a musical comedy?

TN: Like "To-kyooo naga-remonoooo", isn't it? But Seijun Suzuki didn't make such scenes intending to make the audience laugh; he did it earnestly to please them. What's wrong with my case is, I reckon, that I make certain scenes actually intending to make people laugh. I guess I'm doing this a bit too seriously.

RS: French people have recently become interested in Seijun Suzuki, they think his films are parodic comedies.

TN: I see what you mean because his films could be interpreted in different ways. They may be seen as parodic comedies today. But, taking that into account, he, Seijun Suzuki, skilfully leads the audience from a state of laughter gradually into the opposite state. His films adeptly include emotions like anger and sorrow in their own ways and manipulate their audiences' minds.

RS: Can you think of around five good examples of strange or erotic Japanese films?

TN: Let me think – first, there are two films called **Kurotokage (Black Lizard)**. One

*Writer Yukio Mishima in Kinji Fukasaku's **Black Lizard** (1968)*

is the relatively famous **Kurotokage** made at the end of the '60s, in which Akihiro Maruyama or Akihiro Miwa – a transvestite – stars[9]. The other is a criminal musical in which a glamorous young lady – she's now middle-aged though – called

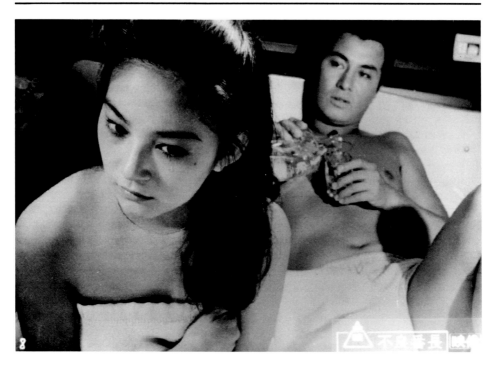

Yukio Noda's **Delinquent Boss**

Machiko Kyo stars[10]. She also appears in Kenji Mizoguchi's films[11]. This first **Kurotokage** is a stylish musical film influenced by 1920s' pulp fiction. There were many bizarre-sexual films produced by Toei in the late '60s/early '70s. For example, Teruo Ishii's **Tokugawa Onna Keizu [Tokugawa Women Bloodline]** and **Onsen Anma Geisha [Hot Springs Geisha, 1968]**. So, as good examples, I would say **Tokugawa Onna Keizu**, **Onsen Anma Geisha** and **Kurotokage**. **Hikisakareta Niso [Violated Nun]** is also one of the bizarre-sexual films. There are films called the **Furyo Bancho [Delinquent Boss]** series, which are Japanese motorbiker films[12]. They were produced by the production company called Toei. Toei made them as Japanese versions of Roger Corman's motorbiker film in which Dennis Hopper and Jack Nicholson star, by interpreting it in their own way – but they turned out as totally unrelated films. They're not like motorbiker films at all. Their characters visit hot springs in different towns and simply shout low-level jokes called *shimoneta* such as *unko* [shit] and *chinchin* [dick]. These many nonsense films are called the **Furyo Bancho** series. They're quite interesting. I don't know if everybody thinks them interesting but, as a Japanese person, I think they are.

RS: Do you think today's Japanese film makers can make such interesting films?

TN: Well – I don't think so. There is a film called **Zatoichi [Blind Swordsman]**. Its hero is a blind masseur and he slashes everything in half with a sword in a flash, which is called *iainuki*. Let's assume that **Zatoichi** doesn't exist, such a film has never been made in Japanese film history. Then, if I proposed a project for a film in which a person slashes everything in half to today's Japanese film makers, they would definitely reject it. So, I suppose Japanese people were a bit more understanding or flexible in the '60s. I don't think it's possible today to make films like **Kozure Ookami** and **Zatoichi**, which have been introduced abroad and seen by many people all over the world. It's not possible because of financial reasons first, and then political reasons as well. That means, due to censorship, the words used in the above films such as *mekura* and *tsunbo* [pejorative words for the blind and the deaf, respectively] are not allowed to be used any more in films. There are many restrictions. So, perhaps it's not possible to make such films today.

RS: What do you think about **Kekko Kamen [Kekko Mask]**?

TN: It's an amusing film. I know the director. His company's called Japan Home. I'm surprised that you know this film. There are three free-standing films in the **Kekko Kamen** series[13]. This might come from my jealousy but I think, if I directed these films, I could make them more amusing. I think what's called an amusing film doesn't mean a film in which simply funny characters make comical movements. Something more – I can't explain it well though. Anyway, **Kekko Kamen** is quite well-known in America.

RS: Yes. Can you think of some other similar films? Something sort of light or childish?

TN: There is a director called Minoru Kawasaki and he's been making **Chikyuboeishojo Iko-chan [Iko, Earth Defender]**. It's a parody of the famous TV programme called *Urutoraman [Ultraman]*, a popular hero series in the '60s and '70s. Every week, the hero fights against many monsters from different planets. Minoru Kawasaki is also making some other films by asking TV stations which broadcast all night for money.

RS: Apart from *Urutoraman*, there is a series of **Reipuman [Rapeman]**, isn't there?

TN: Oh yes, **Reipuman**. I'm impressed that you're familiar with these films. There is a category called *buishine*. Films categorised as *buishine* are not allowed to be shown on TV because they're too sexually explicit. But they're not adult videos; they're in the middle.

RS: Such films are not for cinema and TV but only for the video market?

TN: Yes, only for the video market. Me, too. I'm working only for the video market at the moment.

RS: How long do films of this type last?

TN: About 70 minutes, I believe.

RS: Yours, too?

TN: Yes. We don't wanna see rape scenes for too long, for 2 hours, do we? The latest **Reipuman**, in which a lady called Kei Mizutani stars – she also appears in one of my works – is a parody of **Batman** films. I like it.

RS: I'm sure it's impossible to make such jokes or such series in Europe.

TN: Why not?

RS: Nobody would invest money because they're too sexual, bizarre and in "bad taste".

TN: Recently, I've been seriously thinking about something. I'm *otaku* [obsessive comics/film fan] myself, but what other *otaku* people make have become less and less interesting. Now, in Japan, a robot animation film called **Evangelion** is currently a great hit.

RS: The bandaged heroine appears?

TN: That's right. Because of her, escorts now embellish parts of their body with bandages whilst working. The heroine's called Ayanami.

RS: It may be because Japanese culture is relatively suitable for fetishism.

TN: Having studied someone's work – such as your medical art, for instance – *otaku* people made **Evangelion** by gathering innumerable details picked from them. As compared to a tree, this film consists of only leaves without a trunk. It's made by piling innumerable small details, or *kusuguri* [tickling] – I can't find a good word in Japanese – which are likely to appeal to intellectuals. This is a parody of everything. There is no substance in it. **Evangelion** had started as a TV series and then it was made into a film. It's been a great success; about 200,000 people have seen it. Besides, apparently 150,000 people saw it on the first day of release; which means, let's say there are 150 cinemas in the whole country, more than 1,000 people went to a cinema which has a seating capacity of only 200. This is amazing.

RS: There's been no interesting major films recently, has there?

TN: Yes, as I said, this year's great hit is **Evangelion**. I don't like it though.

RS: It's an animation, isn't it?

TN: Yes, it is.

RS: What about films which are not animation?

TN: Let me think – those showing are not that appealing. **Gozira [Godzilla]**'s finished. **Gamera** is now on but it's nothing special[14]. It doesn't make me feel like going to see it.

RS: Even though **Gozira** is a major film, it's for rather young people.

TN: For children.

RS: Are there any interesting major films for adults?

TN: Well, I don't know what's being made, first of all. What are people making? Apparently, Juzo Itami's[15] new film is coming up; it doesn't interest me so much. What else – Kinji Fukasaku is now making a new film. I don't know which film, but I've heard he's making one. Japanese films – ah, Teruo Ishii is making a new film called **Nejishiki**. It's based on the work, *Nejishiki*, of a cartoonist, Tsuge – I don't remember his first name – who's famous in relation to a Japanese underground comic called *Garo*. This would be interesting as directed by Teruo Ishii.

RS: I reckon you're enjoying most being *otaku* in Japanese underground culture.

TN: Well, I don't wanna remain underground. There is subculture and main culture, and I don't wanna remain as one of the subculture at all. Of course, I'd like to appear in the mainstream. More and more people who like subculture are coming close to me. They nestle close to me saying "Nakano-san", and all of them are weird. I often think "You must be sick. Take balanced nourishment, vitamins too, and become healthy, then come to me." I don't like people intending to be underground. They often tend to believe that they've been completed. They're still far too green. I'd rather enjoy talking to elderly people. In education since the war, we've been taught that it had been a dark age before the war. There were military policemen and if you carelessly said something bad about Japan, you were arrested and tortured by them. As one of my favourites, there is a film called **Oshidori Utagassen [Duck Song Contest]**. It's a musical, samurai musical film. It was made in Showa 14 [1940], which means it was made just before Japan rushed into the Second World War. Besides, its music is swing jazz. When Japan was about to start the war against America, there were people making this musical film using swing jazz. It wasn't being made in an underground subculture, but was going to be introduced openly to the whole country. There was a samurai musical film using American music made just before Japan rushed into the Second World War; which means it mightn't have been such a horrible time. Of course, for some left-wing people and communists, it must have been a dark age and, once the war had started, people must have suffered from air raids and stuff; but, I think, it might have been not that bad a time. What I'm trying to say, is that the conceited old men and women of today used to be stupid in a way; chatting at a café and thinking mainly about how to get girls. I'd like to listen to these people, who used to be called "modern boys" and "modern girls". I know that, even if I listened to young people, what they talk about would be more or less the same, at the age of 20 or before 30. I've been recently thinking that what people at the age of 50, 60, or even 70, 80 talk about would be more interesting.

RS: I've heard today's Japanese women's mentality has changed. What do you think about it?

TN: Well, compared to female students of ten years ago, people called *kogyaru* [high school girls] haven't got a sort of curiosity. They don't think about going to different countries so much. Also, they don't much try to talk to different people and make them laugh. Instead, they stay only in Shibuya, having things like *keitai* [mobile phone], *Purikura* ["Print Club"] and a strange game called *tamagochi* [cyber pets], which has been in fashion. They could go on an expedition to other towns and listen to different people. When we were students, not so many but certain small numbers of people, were doing such things. These girls can't speak English, first of all. I reckon today's young people, or teenagers, will grow old surprisingly quickly; they'd soon become old. They haven't got friends, they don't study, and they're not smart. Today's young people have got no alternatives. By that I mean they're rushing in a single straight line. But situations change quickly in the world. Then, those rushing may find themselves in a disadvantageous position; they may fall straight off a precipice. People in the past had more different ideas, so that, if one group failed, another group could back them up; but now everybody is rushing in a single straight line. I wonder, when a situation has changed, if *kogyaru* or young people have the guts or power to fight against it. No, I don't think they have. They'd grow old surprisingly quickly and soon get married, then become very conservative, inflexible office workers or something like that.

RS: Then, what kind of people see your films?

TN: People who see my films are the abnormal [laughs]. Bizarre people. They look like me: fat, wearing glasses, greasy, with a shiny face, and always eating something. I'm surprised that people who come to me saying "Nakano-san, I've seen all your films," all look just like me. Everybody has a beard and round glasses. So, I feel as if I was shut up in a distorted mirror. I feel I'm dripping with sweat.

RS: Is it like the mirror in Orson Welles' **Lady From Shanghai** [USA, 1948]?

TN: Or like the mirror in Bruce Lee's **Enter The Dragon** [USA, 1973].

RS: Well, thank you very much for your time.

TN: Thanks to you.

Exorsister

1 • The **Uratsukidoji** or **Exorsister** films are: **Hakui Jigoku-hen (White Uniform Hell,** 1994); **Daiinshin Fukkatsu-hen (Rebirth Of The Great Lust God,** 1994); **Joyou Senmenki-hen (Bitch With 1,000 Faces,** 1995); and **Makai Gakuen (Demon School,** 1995). The following description (from the U.S. *Mind Candy* catalog) ably captures the **Exorsister** flavour: *"Girls bullying and sexually humiliating each other for lunch money, vampire king who becomes Godzilla-like urchin, masturbating aliens, beautiful princesses trapped by hundreds of penisoids, leather biker rebel schoolgirls, laser sex morphing aliens, Amazon bitch boot wrestling, flying fierce crucifix jingling, papacy, humiliated nurses and tub money bath taboos".*

2 • **Lend A Child, Lend An Arm,** first in the **Lone Wolf With Cub** series [see chapter 3, note 6]. **Shogun Assassin** is actually the US title of a version of the second instalment **Baby Cart At The River Styx,** edited together with 12 minutes of its predecessor, dubbed and overlaid with an electronic score. Produced by Roger Corman's New World in 1981, the resulting film is an odd but entertaining hybrid, consisting mostly of non-stop blood-spurting action sequences (it has been condemned as a "video nasty" in the UK).

3 • Kenji Misumi, born Kyoto in 1921, joined Nikkatsu in 1941 before moving to Daiei. Almost all his films have been *jidai-geki*, and include **Halo Of Heat Haze** (1959), **Return Of Majin** (1966), and **Devil's Temple** (1969). He directed some of the better **Zatoichi** and **Kyoshiro Nemuri** films – including **Kyoshiro Nemuri: Flaming Sword** (1965) and **Zatoichi's Bloody Path** (1967) – and his entries in the **Lone Wolf With Cub** series are generally considered to be the apotheosis of the genre.

4 • Ichikawa, who also appeared in such *chambara* films as **Band Of Assassins** (1962), **Third Shadow** (1963), and **Lone Wolf** (1966), died prematurely aged 37 after appearing in 12 episodes of **Kyoshiro Nemuri**.

5 • Christianity was first brought to Japan by visiting Portuguese during the 1540s. After 1549, the Shogunate ordered the destruction of all churches and the deportation of all missionaries. Christians were persecuted on a mass scale, being crucified, beheaded, boiled in oil or burnt at the stake if they would not renounce their beliefs (as graphically depicted in such films as Toei's **Joy Of Torture 2** [see chapter 3, note 5]).

6 • **Daibosatsu-toge (Great Bodhisattva Pass)** was actually made in 1935. Director Hiroshi Inagaki followed with **Great Bodhisattva Pass II** in 1936. Tomu Uchida remade **Great Bodhisattva Pass** in 1957, and followed with two sequels in 1958 and 1959. Kenji Misumi directed **Daibosatsu-toge I** and **II** (known in the West as **Satan's Sword**) in 1960. Kihachi Okamoto's 1966 version (known as **Sword Of Doom**) starred Toshiro Mifune.

7 • **Spiral Zone** won first prize at the 1996 Freakzone trash film festival in Lille, northern France. The jury was composed of Virginie Despentes, punk author of ultra-violent novels, Vuillemin, a famous erotic cartoonist, Jack Stevenson, film critic and collector of incredibly strange films (who praised **Spiral Zone** as being "supremely politically incorrect"), and Romain Slocombe, the pioneer of medical art.

*Seijun Suzuki's **Tokyo Drifter***

8 • **Tokyo Drifter** (1965) is the tale of a *yakuza* member who moves from town to town when his gang breaks up, but is stalked and driven into a final confrontation by a rival gunman. Suzuki actually made one more film for Nikkatsu (**Branded To Kill**) before being sacked.

9 • Directed by Kinji Fukasaku in 1968.

10 • Directed by Umeji Inoue in 1962.

11 • Kenji Mizoguchi (1898–1956) was an actor for Nikkatsu before becoming a director in 1922. His main theme was the suffering and sacrifice of women, his best-known films include the ghostly **Tales Of The Pale Moon After Rain** (1953).

12 • Comprising around 16 films shot between 1968 and 1972, the **Delinquent Boss** (*aka* **Wolves Of The City**) series chronicles the adventures of a tough, teenage biker gang known as *Capone*. Main directors on the series were Yukio Noda and Makoto Naito. Nikkatsu Studios responded with their own cycle of female biker movies, **Noraneko Rokku (Alleycat Rock, 1970–72)**. Takayuki Miyagawa's **Boso Sekkusu-zoko (Biker's Race To Hell**, 1973) depicted two rival bike gangs warring at a coastal resort. In 1975 Teruo Ishii directed **Bakuhatsu! Bosozoku (Detonation! Violent Riders)**, starring Sonny Chiba in a bike gang tale which inspired two sequels. In 1976 Toei distributed Mitsuo Yanagimachi's biker documentary **God Speed You: Black Emperor!** with great success; but the best biker movie probably remains Sogo Ishii's apocalyptic **Crazy Thunder Road** [see chapter 8].

13 • **Kekko Kamen: Eiga (Kekko Mask: The Movie**, 1991); **Kekko Kamen (Kekko Mask,** 1993); **Kekko Kamen Koi: 3 (Kekko Mask In Love,** 1995); all directed by Tomo Akiyama [see also chapter 3, note 17].

14 • **Gamera** (1965) marked the first appearance of the eponymous heroic creature, a giant flying turtle created by Daiei Studios in response to Toho's **Godzilla** [see also chapter 6, note 6]. Gamera has since returned in several sequels. A new series was launched in 1995 with **Gamera Vs Gyaos: Decisive Air Battle**, followed in 1996 by **Gamera 2: Advent Of Legion**.

15 • Former actor Juzo Itami's films as director are vapid and mainstream, and include **Ososhiki (Funeral**, 1984); **Tampopo** (1987); and **Marusa No Onna (Lady Tax Officer,** 1987). He reportedly committed suicide in December 1997.

PUNK GENERATION

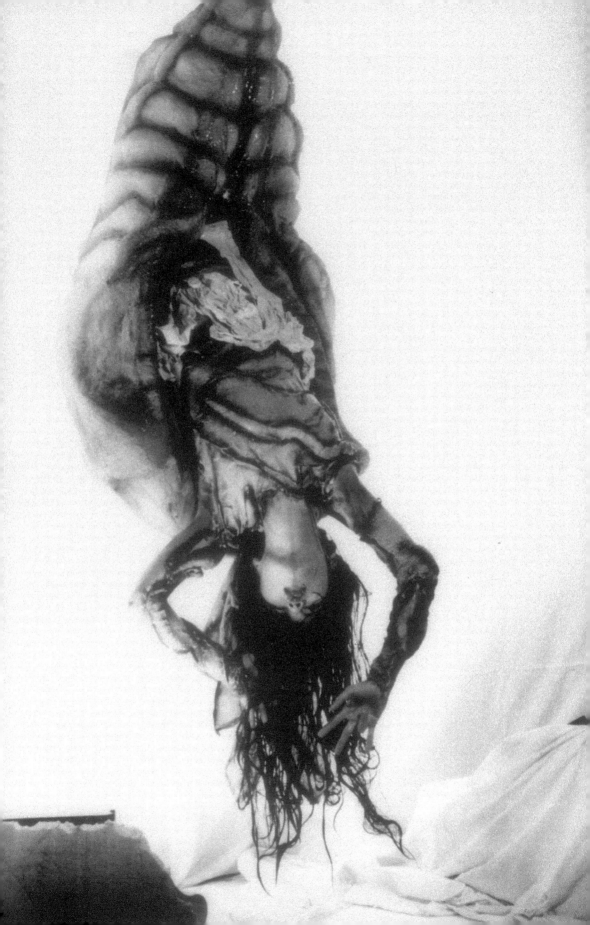

NOTES ON THE JAPANESE UNDERGROUND

"Surrounded by a dozen pigeons. Makoto feeds them. Makoto slowly takes out a pipe and beats the pigeons to death. He lays and hums a tune while observing the dead birds. In sight, the sleeping homeless people of Kamagasaki. Makoto rips off the pigeons' heads and trashes them. Location, Jan-Jan Yokocho."
—From the script of Yoshihiko Matsui's **Noisy Requiem** (1989)

As with most world cinemas, the seeds of Japanese experimental film-making can be traced back nearly as far as the origins of the artform, at least as far as Teinosuke Kinugasa's surrealistic **Kurutta Ippeiji (Pages Of Madness**, 1926). Japanese cinema has been a cinema of poetry and violence from its outset, a mixture that proved appealing to critics and audiences worldwide. Yasujiro Ozu's films of atmospheric quietness, Akira Kurosawa's large-scale dramas, Nagisa Oshima's challenges of Japanese tradition and Hiroshi Teshigahara's existential interrogatives have long since become major fixtures in international cinema history. But it is only since the 1960s, with the rebellious breakaway of Koji Wakamatsu from Nikkatsu [see chapter 2], that the rigid codes of the Japanese film industry have begun to be questioned, broken and abolished. This chapter concerns experimental film-makers working outside the studio system, and modern film-makers who, despite the advent of video, still pursue their individual visions on celluloid.

New Wave directors like Oshima, Teshigahara, Shinoda, Hani, Masumura and Imamura enjoyed mainstream success into the '60s[1], a decade at whose subterranean epicentre remains Koji Wakamatsu. While Seijun Suzuki introduced experimentation into mainstream exploitation cinema and was fired by Nikkatsu as a result, Wakamatsu remained not only independent and autonomous, but resolutely underground by dint of his uncompromising depictions of sado-sexual violence; the other directors on his axis, such as Atsushi Jiku Yamatoya, Masao

*Katsu Kanai's **The Deserted Reef***

Adachi, Osamu Yamashita, Kazuo Komizu and Isao Okishima [see chapter 2, note 5], pursued experimental and/or political tangents which flowered on the cusp of the '70s with the appearance of such films as Toshio Matsumoto's landmark **Funeral Procession Of Roses**[2], Katsu Kanai's oneiric **The Deserted Reef**, and Shuji Terayama's outrageous **Emperor Tomato Ketchup** [see chapter 2, note 12].

The origins of what may be termed the "pure underground" strand of Japanese cinema are equally recent, tracing back to the birth of the '60s. It was then that the *Ao No Kai* (Club Blue) was formed by a collective of directors and cinematographers with a common experimental leaning (particularly toward *cinéma vérité* and documentary); these included Yoichi Higashi, Kazuo Kuroki, Hisaya Iwasa, Shinsuke Ogawa, Tatsuo Suzuki, and Noriaki Tsuchimoto.

One of the best-known early experimental film-makers was Taka Iimura, whose prolific (and often erotic) output includes **Ai (Love)** and **Peep Show**. Iimura also collaborated with avant-garde theatrical troupes such as Hijikata's, producing such works as **Bara No Iro Dansu (Rose Dance**, 1966), which depicts "the birth of a virgin from a transvestite's belly". This fusion of film and theatre predates the work of Katsu Kanai and Shuji Terayama[3]. Iimura's later films became more abstract, studies in movement and light such as **+ ET – (From 1 To 60 Seconds,** 1973). Working in a similar vein was Kenji Kanesaka, whose films include **Hopscotch** (1967) and **Rosebud** (1968). The painter/animator Takehiko Kamei also produced US-affiliated films with English titles, including **Tale Of Moon** and **Smile**. Kohei Ando (**Oh My Mother**, 1969; **The Sons**, 1973) was the purveyor of a poetic, homoerotic cinema inspired by Jean Cocteau. Yoichi Takabayashi produced many experimental 8mm and 16mm films, including **Namu** (1959), **Ishikoro (A Stone**, 1960) and **Suna (Dunes**, 1963). Like many of his peers, he has often had to compromise in order to finance his career, producing longer commercial movies like **Sekka Tomurai Zashi (The Tattooed Woman**, 1982). Nobuhiko Obayashi's films

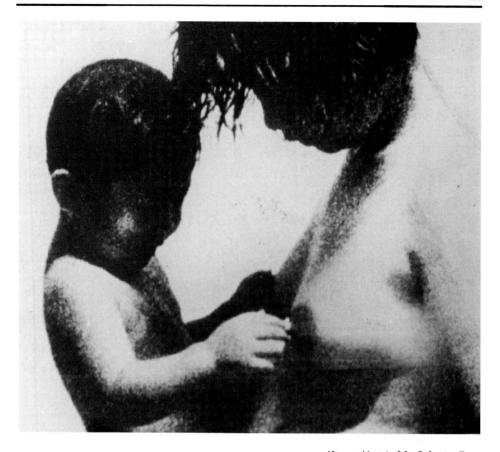

Kazuo Hara's **My Private Eros**

(such as **Katami [The Thought Beast, 1961]** and **Tabetahito [The Devoured Man,
1963])** are bizarrely-themed works featuring pixillation and deconstructions of
time/space. Obayashi later produced **House** (1977), his psychedelic version of the
Japanese ghost/horror movie. Other notable avant-garde directors of this period
include Sakumi Hagiwara, Michio Okabe, and Teruo Okumura.

Masato Hara has produced many experimental films since 1968, with titles
like **The Rhetoric Of Cellophane.** Kazuo Hara, working in 16mm, produced
Gokushiteki Eros Renka (My Private Eros: Love Song, 1974), an intimate cinematic
diary of his relationship with the woman with whom he conceived a child, also
featured in the film. Hara's other films include **Sayonara C.P. (Goodbye Cerebral
Palsy, 1972),** a documentary on the mentally handicapped. Yoshimitsu Morita has
produced dozens of short 8mm and Super-8 movies since 1970, films such as
Posi-?, Hex, Sky, Mother, Nude, and **Film.** He progressed straight to 35mm in
1981, finding success in 1983 with the satirical **Kazoku Geemu (Family Games).**
That same year Masashi Yamamoto directed **Yami No Carnival (Carnival Of Night),**
an unflinching descent into the nocturnal inferno of Shinjuku with a soundtrack
by the punk band Jagatara. Sex, drugs and nihilism combine in this violent 16mm
apocalypse, which juxtaposes a woman's cruise, gun in pocket, of the streets while
below, in an industrial labyrinth, a crazed engineer pores over maps of the city's

Masashi Yamamoto's **Carnival Of Night**

supply system to determine the single point where a bomb will devastate the whole of Shinjuku. The biggest recent explosion in the Japanese underground – resulting from the convergence of "post-punk" strands of noise music, cyber-aesthetics and Super-8 cine-culture[4] – had been well and truly detonated.

Inspired chiefly by Koji Wakamatsu, the "punk generation" of young film-makers forged ahead using Super-8 and 16mm, utilising their friends plus co-opted musicians, junkies and petty criminals as actors, and deriving their films' stories and spirit from urban fringe cultures such as *bosuzoku* (bikers), *chima* (youth gangs), and the punk music and drugs scene. As Masashi Yamamoto has commented: "We had a sense of physicality and not of intellectuality, which made us different from people like Oshima. We had no contact to the experimental avant-garde either. We wanted to show our films at places where people would see them, not in academies. We arranged screenings in strip clubs and abandoned buildings. We had warehouse shows where a strip show came first, the movies second, and a punk rock concert lasted the rest of the night."[5] At the forefront of this movement was Sogo Ishii, whose excessively violent biker movie **Crazy Thunder Road** (1980) was the first film to emerge from this loose scene and receive nationwide attention and notoriety[6]. Toei Studios duly picked it up for a major release, enhancing it to 35mm, while Eirin marvelled over its artistic merits in contrast to its nihilistic, anti-social stance. Ishii's fellow film-makers perceived this success as a starting-point to finally get real. Masashi Yamamoto sums up the spirit of the times: "I thought: Ishii is a fool. But if he could get a movie out like that – I could too. I could do it better."[7]

Sogo Ishii's **Crazy Thunder Road**

Sogo Ishii's **Burst City**

Ishii followed up **Crazy Thunder Road** with **Bakuretsu Toshi (Burst City,** 1982), almost two hours' worth of high-octane action and weirdness. Despite its obvious budget limitations, this loud and angry anti-social glimpse into the future flies by like a hit of nitrous oxide. A pair of odd-looking individuals come to the big, ugly city in their motorbike and sidecar. Meanwhile, all the punked-out, spiky-haired kids are dancing at the Asian version of CBGB, dressed in their oddest leathers, and drag racing around Japan. Much of the film is spent on the misadventures of a rock band living in a factory-style squat, and the film ends in pandemonium when the drag racers clash with activists protesting the construction of a nuclear power plant. Ishii next made **Hanbun Ningen (Half Human**, 1983), a documentary on German noise band Einstürzende Neubauten. The film contains live concert footage intermixed with shots of the band and Ishii's video for ½ *Mensch*.[8]

Yoshihiko Matsui's **Pig-Chicken-Suicide**

In 1981, Kyoto-based film-maker Yoshihiko Matsui premiered his personal, violently poetic take on minorities in Japan, **Pig-Chicken-Suicide**. This film depicts two Koreans living in Kyoto, and their love which gets torn apart due to racial discrimination in an environment that refuses to accept anybody non-Japanese. Even some Japanese people have to suffer this prejudice – the "untouchable" *burakumin* people working in the slaughterhouses. Matsui then produced **Tsuito No Zawameki (Noisy Requiem**, 1989) – the biggest-ever collaborative effort of the Japanese underground scene. Everybody from Sogo Ishii to Masashi Yamamoto to Shinya Tsukamoto worked on this film, from a deranged script which many thought to be unfilmable (it depicts the grinding daily life of several social

*Yoshihiko Matsui's **Noisy Requiem***

outcasts in Kyoto, focusing on the plastic doll-loving, mass-murdering Makoto, employed as gutter-cleaner by a pair of incestuous midgets). **Noisy Requiem** in fact proved to be one of the biggest independent successes on the domestic market.

*Katsuhiro Otomo's **World Apartment Horror***

Katsuhiro Otomo's **World Apartment Horror** (1990) presents post-punk horror as a young gangster is given the task of clearing a house of its occupants within a week. Otomo hints at black magic and paranoia as the hapless youth comes face to face with the World Apartment's weird, grotesque tenants.

Kyoichi Komoto's **Tokyo Crash**

Urban alienation is also the theme of Kyoichi Komoto's rough and nihilistic **Tokyo Crash** (1997), in which a traumatized ex-soldier returning from a UN mission to some unnamed jungle terrain has nobody to come home to, and is only kept going by the obsessive idea of returning a dead comrade's watch to his girlfriend. He never meets the girl, only finding out that she is wanted for theft. He finally falls in love with another girl, Yuri, who he meets on his search – which proves to be a fatally wrong decision. Yuri is heavily in debt, and persuades the ex-soldier to take on a job as a hired assassin. He bungles the planned hit terribly...

Another cutting-edge modern film-maker – working largely in Super-8 – is the 24-year-old Kenji Onishi, whose **Squareworld** (1995) could be considered on one level to be an almost pure experimental film, although it also contains an abundance of the classic ingredients of exploitation cinema: sex, violence and murder. A drug-addicted man kidnaps a young woman, holds her prisoner, and eventually kills her and disposes of her body. **Squareworld** is a stark, amoral work of which one critic has said: "Onishi has erected a monument of cruel celluloid on the North Pole of the cinema world". Onishi's short **A Burning Star** caused one of

Shinya Tsukamoto's **Tetsuo**

the biggest scandals in recent Japanese cinema history when it was premiered at the 1996 Image Forum Festival. The film depicts the cremation of a human body, filmed right through the oven's window. The flames create a strange beauty, and the close-ups look rather like shots from some planet on fire, than an earthly crematorium. When Image Forum's curators, however, found that it was one of Onishi's relatives who was burning, even they felt that this was a little too much.

Meanwhile Kenichi Iwamoto, somewhat of an outsider even within the independent scene, deals in his **Kikuchi** (1992) less with violence than with grinding, urban desperation. Laundry worker Kikuchi is practically incapable of any kind of social interaction, and his main activity is stalking the check-out girl from the local supermarket. When he discovers that she is the girlfriend of his nasty new co-worker, Kikuchi is finally forced into action.

The most resonant strand of the new Japanese cult cinema stems from the cyberpunk trope most clearly defined by former Ishii and Matsui collaborator Shinya Tsukamoto's **Tetsuo** (**The Iron Man**, 1989). **Tetsuo**, one of the best-known Japanese films in the West, has lost none of its power. Shot in black and white 16mm, and lasting some 67 minutes, Tsukamoto's vision is one of man into machine, a fusion which throws up such unforgettable images as the protagonist trying to fuck his girlfriend with a power-drill penis. Eventually the girl is infected by the same disease, and the two mutants pursue each other through Tokyo in exhilarating sequences of pixillated insanity set to a pounding industrial score by Chu Ishikawa. Tsukamoto offers no explanation for the film's events, preferring to present his scenario as a living nightmare – although various interpretations, including an attack on the Japanese "salaryman", have been imposed by others. In 1991 Tsukamoto produced **Tetsuo 2 – Body Hammer**, a feature-length, colour

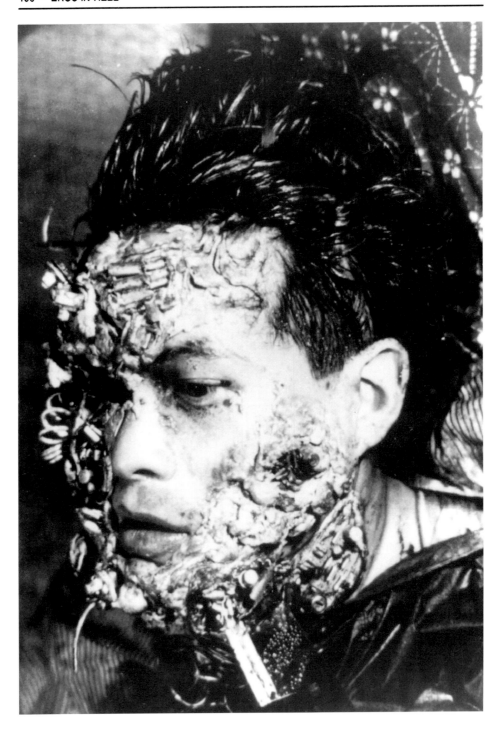

Shinya Tsukamoto's **Tetsuo**

reprise of his earlier film. Sadly, the director here chose to trammel his original vision with a "logical" storyline which – despite the film's occasional bursts of

Shigeru Izumiya's **Death Powder**

fantastic imagery – ultimately served to dilute the experience.[9]

Predating **Tetsuo** by 3 years, Shigeru Izumiya's **Death Powder** (1986) may be seen as an early entry into the cyberpunk arena. Izumiya, a former protest musician, turned to experimental cinema in the 1980s and **Death Powder** is his third film. With all the trademarks of cyberpunk cinema – an industrial *milieu*, stolen android, mutant sect (called The Scar People), amputation and extreme body morphing, futuristic hardware, rock/noise soundtrack and multiple camera tricks – **Death Powder** still compels the viewer, despite its non-narrative structure and restless experimental technique. The result is undeniably hallucinatory, with the viewer best advised to sit back and absorb on a primal level the swathes of grotesque superimposed imagery and sound, glyphs of light striated across the shifting screen, and liquid psychogeometry of "cult violence color".

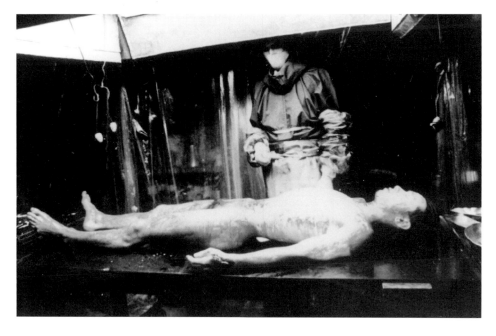

Kei Fujiwara's **Organ**

Kei Fujiwara's **Organ**

Fast-forwarding a decade to 1996, **Organ** by Kei Fujiwara (who played the female lead in **Tetsuo**) is the latest (and surely the ultimate) in a line of independent productions in which extremes of violence, destruction and mutation to the human body are investigated. **Organ** is distanced from gore videos like **Guinea Pig** by Fujiwara's pedigree (a former stage actress, she heads her own avant-garde theatre Organ Vital, where *Organ* was originally a play) and the fact that she is a female film-maker, one of only a handful in Japan. But this film is as extreme as any ever made in its depictions of a ring of depraved body-part dealers, amputation and vivisection, cruel experiments, schoolgirl murder, weird sex, mutilation, metamorphosis, rape, and a blood-drenched climax which is positively surreal in its violent scope. Painting in blood and guts, Fujiwara creates a cinematic butchershop in which the casual viewer may find his sensibilities dismembered on a flat meat, post-cyberpunk slab.

Although he now distances himself from the cooling melting-pot of cyberpunk [see following interview], film-maker Shojin Fukui is regarded as another major player in the genre. After his first, extreme, Super-8 film **Gerrorist**, Fukui produced **Caterpillar** in 1988. In this disturbing, 40-minute opus, which often resembles the home-movie of a psychopath as opposed to an actual piece of cinema, several teenage kids wander, run and tumble through a menacing Tokyo cityscape, each of them isolated, their aims unknown, each haunted by their own particular mental deviations. But it is Fukui's next film, **Pinocchio 964** (1992), which really aligns him with the cyber avant-garde. Pinocchio 964 is a brand of sex cyborg, created by a company to service sexually-frustrated older women. A new 964 (played by Hage Suzuki with a kinetic, punk-Noh performance of crazed intensity) falls short of standard, is lobotomised and thrown out into the streets

Shojin Fukui's **Pinocchio 964**

where he wanders without purpose until adopted by Himiko, an enigmatic young streetgirl (an ex-nurse?) who lives in a deserted factory. Slowly the cyborg regains

Shojin Fukui's **Rubber's Lover**

his powers of speech and memory, and with them unbridled anger against his creators, who he tracks down in order to exact a terrible revenge.

In the course of the story, Fukui indulges his custom motifs of bodily excretion (copious vomiting and haemorrhaging), aberrant sex, and madness in claustrophobic industrial settings. One particularly impressive, extended sequence is Pinocchio's careering headlong flight through the streets, back alleys and wastelands of Tokyo back to the factory of his origin. The cyborg's final act of retribution is cataclysmic and involves graphic eviscerations and transmutations until all the protagonists are either dead or mortally insane. Like a trip through the intestines of a psychotropic beast, **Pinocchio 964** is the equal of **Tetsuo** in its invocation of a new super-reality where meat, metal and madness compact to coronate the putrid anus of a black sun planet.

Fukui followed **Pinocchio 964** with the startling **Rubber's Lover** in 1996. Filmed in black and white 16mm, **Rubber's Lover** depicts a world of psychic experimentation and physical destruction. Four scientists are working in a secret lab on a "rubber unit" designed to destroy the human spirit and causing a continual "trip". But the kidnapped guinea pig cannot cope with the toughness of the experiment, and funds are running out. One of the researchers, Shimizu, becomes the last guinea pig to complete the experiment. Just as he loses his mind in the rubber suit, beautiful secretary Kiku is coming over to announce the termination of the project. Her appearance – and savage rape by one of the technicians – provokes reactions in Shimizu nobody had foreseen.

With exquisite cinematography and a lacerating electronic score, **Rubber's Lover** is a work of severe madness, presenting a relentless alternating array of weird, industrial, sexy and graphically gory images; a giant, fibrillating eyeball,

美しく、
破壊的な
伝説の誕生…。

福居ショウジン監督作品

ラバーズ・ラヴァー

'96年～'97年全国主要都市劇場公開作品

exploding bodies and rain-showers of blood, cannibalism, physical abuse by penetrative fetishistic machinery, telepathic orgasm, projectile vomiting, and stroboscopic glimpses of intense visceral carnage.

At the end of **Rubber's Lover**, Kiku eliminates the remaining scientist and escapes, ending up sitting in a busy Tokyo street – a direct reprise of the opening post-title shot of **Pinocchio 964**. This cyclical device seems to indicate that Fukui has completed his investigations into the cyberpunk universe, and he has indeed indicated that his next project will involve a virus [see interview], perhaps signalling a move away from technology toward the purely biological world of Kei Fujiwara's **Organ**. Whatever its themes, the next film by Shojin Fukui will undoubtedly be one of the most highly-anticipated events in the Japanese underground.

Shojin Fukui was interviewed by Romain Slocombe in April 1997, at Mr Fukui's office in Ikejiri-Ohashi, Tokyo.

ROMAIN SLOCOMBE: You made a film called **Gerrorist**. It is a very extreme film, isn't it? Did you intend it to be that extreme?
SHOJIN FUKUI: Yes. That was my initial intention.
RS: Does it somehow reflect your feelings?
SF: I think so. I made it in a suppressed situation, so that the completed film naturally reflected my destructive impulses.
RS: Do you think that those impulses are a reaction to Japanese society? Do you ever have an urge to destroy it?
SF: Sure I do. I always want to destroy something entirely and reconstruct it from scratch. That is my objective in the work I create.
RS: Did you make any short films before **Gerrorist**?
SF: I made a few shorts as a student, but **Gerrorist** was the first film that I shot out of a desire to work with the medium of film.
RS: What format did you use for that film?
SF: 8mm. It advanced past the preliminary stage of a certain Japanese film competition.
RS: When was that?
SF: In 1987. After that, I made another 8mm called **Caterpillar,** and then **Pinocchio 964.**
RS: What is the theme of **Pinocchio**?
SF: "Nothing". Attaining the state of nothing in Zen. I wanted crew, actors and audience all to feel that. To feel the tension building up to climax, to the point of ecstasy, where one feels transported.
RS: I saw your **Rubber's Lover** last year and was very impressed by the beauty of its expressionistic images. What is the message of that film?
SF: What I wanted to depict in that film is a new power human beings possess, in other words a hidden, unrealized potential power in ourselves. I wanted to show the impact such power has when it is finally released. I also wanted to make something different from ordinary psychic movies and to express violence in a way that it has never been depicted before. Creating something that has never existed before is one of my main objectives in making films.
RS: Do you think the theme of fusion of man and machine, also depicted in **Tetsuo** by Shinya Tsukamoto, reverberates for the present younger generation in Japan?

*Shojin Fukui's **Rubber's Lover***

SF: Well, we seem to share similar feelings about this theme, so I would say that we were strongly influenced by similar movies, music and so on. The fusion of a man and a machine inspires me, that coolness and ecstasy of a body melting into a machine. It's been called "cyberpunk", but I tried to make **Rubber's Lover** in a way that excluded a cyberpunk element.

RS: Was **Rubber's Lover** well received by mainstream critics?

SF: They were poles apart in their opinions: one had a very visceral negative reaction to it, and another had a very positive one and told me that he got very high watching it. The soundtrack is highly regarded by music critics in Japan. But those critics who mainly review entertainment movies had a lukewarm reaction.

RS: What did you think about their lukewarm reaction? Did it make you even more certain of your decision to pursue your career as an underground filmmaker?

SF: In Japan, the term "underground" doesn't exist. We use the term "Indies". And there isn't a distinction made between Indies and "commercial film", because an Indies can easily become a commercial film once it becomes a success. That's why I was very glad to see **Rubber's Lover** appreciated as an underground film, but I will also be very glad to have a wider audience see my film.

RS: How is **Rubber's Lover** distributed?

SF: We worked with a distribution company for theatres in Tokyo. In other areas, a production company is responsible for the distribution.

RS: How did you manage to raise the funds for the production budget?

SF: Mr. Kobayashi and I invested jointly in it.

RS: Did it take you a long time to shoot the film?

SF: Yes, it did.

RS: Do you tend to focus on small details?

SF: I think I do, but I like a more radical approach as well. I usually do not do a lot of detailed preparation for a shoot. I just start shooting sort of guerrilla style. I'll get on the subway and just start to shoot, something like that. I like that style of shooting best. I feel I'm good at that style. We did a **Rubber's Lover** shoot in a confined space with actors and crew. In order to keep a high level of tension between all involved, no one was allowed to speak a single word during the shoot.

RS: Is the script for **Rubber's Lover** your original screenplay?

SF: Yes, it is.

RS: I've heard that even native Japanese speakers have difficulty understanding all of the lines. Is that intentional? Do you like that style?

SF: **Rubber's Lover** happened to be made in that style. The actors spoke their lines in such a high tension that the audience could not figure out what they were saying. But if you see the film two or three times, you will eventually understand it. I didn't want to make an entertainment movie but rather the sort of film which requires you to watch it several times in order to understand it, which reflects the extreme energy and effort that went into the creation of it. It is a totally different approach from making an ordinary drama or story.

RS: Have you been a big fan of the movies since you were a child? What kind of movies did you like as a child?

SF: Yes, I've always been a big fan of movies. I remember seeing all the Disney movies as a kid. There was a movie theatre next door. I watched all the animated movies by Toei. When I was 15 or 16 I began to see movies consciously. That was when American New Cinema re-ran at the theatre and I saw all of them.

RS: What is your favourite Japanese film?

SF: I like Yuzo Kawashima's **Suzaki Paradise** the best[10]. I also like **Yaju [Wild**

Beast] by Sadaji Aoyama. He suffered from stomach cancer, yet managed to finish shooting it even though he was coughing up blood. I knew I wanted to make movies when I saw that film.

RS: How do you like the series of bizarre movies made in the '60s and '70s?

SF: I like them very much. They had a huge influence on me. I go crazy over those "splatter" horror movies, especially the ones that have no narrative consistency. My favourite is Tobe Hooper's **Texas Chainsaw Massacre** [USA, 1974], which had a huge impact on me. When it was first released in Japan, it was partially cut and re-edited. Then I saw the original. It was great. It is the greatest. I have never seen any films that surpass it in madness, splatter, and horror. It was and still is a very special film for me. I was also very influenced by **Possession** [France/Germany, 1981] by Andrzej Zulawski.

RS: Which director's work do you see as having a similar feel to yours?

SF: Peter Jackson's early works.[11]

RS: The expression of eroticism, the grotesque and violence in Japanese culture seems to me very unique compared to Western culture. What do you think?

SF: I enjoy watching those films as part of an audience, but, as a filmmaker, I want to explore my own, different methods of expression.

RS: In the last scene of **Rubber's Lover**, the girl is sitting at the station with a blank look on her face as people pass in front of her. What is your message, in that scene?

SF: She's acquired unwanted psychic power and she's forced into a situation where she has to use it. She has lost both her past and her future. That's the emptiness on her face.

RS: Does the emptiness have something to do with contemporary Japanese society?

SF: Definitely. However, no one thinks it is empty. Neither do I. But to those who view it from the outside, it is empty. It is complicated.

RS: Do you find that contemporary Japanese mentality is changing?

SF: The change is taking place not only in Japan but everywhere, I think.

RS: The younger generation in Japan, and especially teenagers referred to as *Ko-gal*, seem to have no interest in art or culture but only in the latest fashion.

SF: That is often pointed out, but when I was younger we had a similar equivalent young group called *Yankee*. In that way it really hasn't changed much. It's just a difference of style and expression, I guess.

RS: Older Japanese films like Kurosawa's made very strong statements in spite of their comparatively low budgets. Now, even with big budgets, great techniques, beautiful photography and all that, they don't seem to be able to make good mainstream movies any more.

SF: It's very sad. Our assistant director has worked in the Japanese commercial film industry and he was very bored. That's why he joined us, to make more interesting films. We hope the films we make are interesting films, that will eventually become successful commercial films as well. Honestly speaking, contemporary Japanese cinema is not exciting at all. What is being done currently is just a remaking of Hollywood's hit movies, completely unchanged, into Japanese movies. It is very easy to do this now because the technology is so advanced. But all those films are just imitations. We should be using these great techniques to express our own unique perspectives and sensibility. I am afraid that we are falling behind other countries in our use of this technology.

RS: What is your next project? And would you like to add some closing comments?

SF: I hope that more people will get to see **Pinocchio**. My next project will be a film that involves a virus. The script is done. It is about a power that could destroy the world, that is breaking out everywhere simultaneously, and everyone discovers their potential for new, psychic powers within themselves. This is a theme I am very interested in right now.

1 • Although some directors were less fortunate. Those falling foul of the stifling studio system (especially Nikkatsu) include, most notably, Kazuo Kawabe (**Hiko Shonen** [**The Delinquents**, 1964]); Kiriro Urayama (**Watashi Ga Suteta Onna** [**The Woman I Abandoned**, 1965]); and Kei Kumai (**Nihon Retto** [**Archipelago Japan**, 1965]).

2 • Toshio Matsumoto was born 1932 in Nagoya. He produced his first short film, **Senkan** (Caisson), in 1956. Other experimental films followed, including **Shiroi Nagai Sen No Kiroku** (**Chronicle Of A Long White Line**, 1962) and **Tsuburekakatta Migi Me No Tame Ni** (**To Become Blind In The Right Eye**, 1968), until his first feature, **Funeral Procession Of Roses**, in 1969 [see also chapter 4, note 11]. **Funeral Procession Of Roses** is an experimental, gay version of *Oedipus Rex*, in which a transvestite nightclub host(ess) in "swinging Shinjuku" (played by Peter) steals the affections of his boss; in the film's climax, the boss realises that Eddie (now his gay lover) is actually his son by the wife he killed years before, and commits suicide in the bathroom. When Eddie discovers this scene, he cuts out his own eyes with a knife.

Toshio Matsumoto's **Pandemonium**

Matsumoto's two other feature-length films, **Pandemonium** and **Jurokusai No Senso** (**War Of The 16-Year-Olds**), were made in 1971 and 1973 respectively. He has since continued to produce short films such as **Andy Warhol/Fukufukusei** (**Andy Warhol/Reproduction**, 1974), **Shiki Soku Ze Ku** (**The Blue Woman**, 1975), and **Black Hole** (1977).

3 • Although Terayama did produce two early 8mm shorts: **Nekogaku** (**Catology**, 1960) and **Ori** (**The Cage**, 1964).

4 • Japan is still the only country with a vital Super-8 scene, as Super-8 is still the most easily accessible medium to aspiring young film-makers. Recent examples are Norichio

Saruyama, who uses the format for his short, rapid-fire fantasies of violence and slime such as **Fat Man And The Octopus** and **Bird Of Paradise**, and Kazuhiro Shirao (**Plastic Model In The Night, Industry And The Sex Doll**, etc).

5 • From an interview by Johannes Schonherr.

6 • **Crazy Thunder Road** is a mean, rough-house road movie, a **Mad Max**-style revenge tale of a man who takes on a group of vicious bikers after they molest and kill his girlfriend. Ishii's first movie was **Koko Daipanikku (High School Big Panic**, 1978), made at the University of Japan.

7 • From an interview by Johannes Schonherr. Yamamoto adds: "In the 1980s we felt suffocated by the middle class. Our movie characters reflected that. They acted out our repressed sides in their own ways, just as the people did we were [hanging] around with. Many of these people couldn't actually take it in the long run, and a couple of them died. Things have changed since then. Much more is possible now, and outsiders have it easier but, on the other hand, they get commercialised. The middle class co-opts them and exploits them for their entertainment value."

Masashi Yamamoto's **Junk Food**

Yamamoto himself has remained with his outlaws. In his most recent film, **Junk Food** (1998), he follows the street people of Tokyo today. It is a much more international bunch of outsiders nowadays populating the fringe zones of the city than back in the days of **Carnival Of Night**, but it is also one that has almost completely lost the contact with its own traditions, be they Japanese or otherwise. Yamamoto's '90s Tokyo is a city in which a corpse can circle around all day long on the Yamanote subway line without anybody even noticing it. **Junk Food** follows one day in the life of several rootless outsiders, both Japanese and foreign, all of them cheating and being cheated, being violent and victims of violence. A junkie girl and her sadistic dope dealer, stylish young *chima* gang members, a desperate Pakistani immigrant, a female Mexican wrestler; all subsisting on cheap Western food, all hanging out at the same anonymous, Western-style places.

8 • Ishii's other films include **Gyaku Funsha Kazoku (Crazy Family, 1984)** the serial killer entry **Angel Dust (1994)**, and **Mizu No Naka No Hachigatsu (August In The Water,** 1995). His most recent is **Yume No Ginga (Labyrinth Of Dreams, 1996)**, a film of refined mysteries concerning Tomiko, a bus company guide who is bored with her ordinary life. One day, a man by the name of Mr Niitaka joins the bus company and Tomiko is assigned to be guide on his bus. All the other women in the company are fascinated by this handsome young man but, from the beginning, Tomiko is suspicious of him. The reason for this is that her best friend, Tsuyako, used to work as a guide on the same bus as Mr Niitaka and was killed in a mysterious accident shortly after becoming the driver's fiancée. And it was Mr Niitaka driving the bus...

*Sogo Ishii's **Labyrinth Of Dreams***

9 • Tsukamoto's next film **Hiroku: Yokai Hanta (Hiroku: Monster Hunting,** 1991) was a total departure, being a rehash of the traditional Japanese ghost story only enlivened by some occasionally impressive special effects and images. Tsukamoto's most recent film, **Tokyo Fist** (1995) was a return to form. Ostensibly about boxing, **Tokyo Fist** investigates a triangular love relationship between a boxer, a salaryman-turned-pugilist, and their mutual body-piercing girlfriend. Rage and mutilation evolve into a bloody symphony of shattered faces, hearts and souls. **Tokyo Fist** was released with Tsukamoto's short film **Denchu Kozo No Boken (Adventures Of Electric Rod Boy,** 1995), echoes of **Tetsuo** in the trippy tale of a boy with an electric rod growing out of his back.

*Shinya Tsukamoto's **Tokyo Fist***

10 • **Suzaki Paradise** was produced in 1956 by Nikkatsu Studios, starring Michiyo Aratama and Tatsuya Mihashi, about the lives of people in a red-light district called Suzaki, in Tokyo. As in most of Kawashima's films, a bridge plays an important role as a background in this film.

11 • New Zealander Peter Jackson's **Bad Taste** (1987: NZ) and **Braindead** (1992: NZ) are low-budget ultra-gore classics.

index

*Films are listed by English titles, except where best/only known in the West by the original Japanese title (e.g. **Onibaba**, **Tetsuo**). Page numbers in bold indicate an illustration.*

ABNORMAL PASSION: RAZOR CASE	72
ABNORMAL WARD: S/M CONSULTATION ROOM	122, 124, **127**
ABNORMAL WARD: TORTURE OF WHITE DRESSES	124
ADULTEROUS LUST	63
ADVENTURE KID	102
ADVENTURES OF ELECTRIC ROD BOY	209
AFTERNOON AFFAIR: KYOTO HOLY TAPESTRY	22, 30
AGE OF NAKEDNESS	29
AI NO BOREI	117, 117, 164
AI NO CORRIDA 60, 76, 103–120, **104**, **105**, **106**, **107**, **108**, **109**, **110**, **111**, **113**, **114**	
AIR HOSTESS CAPTURED BY SEX-SADIST	75
A.K.A. SERIAL KILLER	60
ALL NIGHT LONG	150, 151
ALLEY CAT ROCK	184
ALONE IN THE NIGHT	102
AN ACTOR'S REVENGE	119
ANDY WARHOL/REPRODUCTION	207
ANGEL DUST	209
ANGEL GUTS: RED DIZZINESS	85
ANGEL GUTS: RED LIGHTNING	85
ANGEL GUTS: RED PORNO	84, **84**, 85
ANGEL OF THE FILTHY BEAST	140
ANGELIC ORGASM, THE	49–50, **51**, **64**, 64
APARTMENT WIFE: AFFAIR IN THE AFTERNOON	15
ARCHIPELAGO JAPAN	207
ATROCITY	142, 151–152, 160
ATTACK OF MU-EMPIRE FROM DEEP SEA	169
AUGUST IN THE WATER	209
AUGUST: SCENT OF EROS	30

BABY CART AT THE RIVER STYX	91–93, **92**, 182
BAND OF ASSASSINS	183
BATTLE GIRL	164
BEAUTIFUL TEACHER IN TORTURE HELL	22, 31
BEAUTY AND THE CYBORGASM	102
BEAUTY AND THE DRAGON	119
BEAUTY REPORTER: LIVE HOOK-UP FOR RAPE	123, **128**
BECAUSE SHE DISOBEYED	75
BED OF VIOLENT DESIRES	72
BEDROOM, THE	132, 133–136, **134**, **135**

BIKER'S RACE TO HELL   184
BIRD OF PARADISE   208
BIRTH OF THE WIZARD   **100**, 100
BLACK HOLE   207
BLACK LIZARD (1962)   95, 175, 176–177
BLACK LIZARD (1968)   3, 95, 119, 175, **176**, 176
BLACK MAGIC WARS   91
BLACK ROSE RISING   15
BLACK SNOW   7–8, 25, 35
BLIND WOMAN'S CURSE   89, 164
BLOOD AND ECSTASY   75
BLOOD IS REDDER THAN THE SUN   60
BLOOD SWORD OF THE 99TH VIRGIN   71
BLUE GIRL   102
BLUE WOMAN, THE   207
BOMBSHELL FUCK   25
BONDAGE COLLECTOR: BIG TITS HUNT   140
BONDAGE M: SKIN FEAST   75
BONDAGE OMEN   102
BOUND FOR PLEASURE   75
BOUNDLESS FUCK HELL   140
BOY   59
BRANDED TO KILL   14, 15, **29**, 29, 184
BRUTALITY OF TORTURED WOMEN   75
BURNING STAR, A   194–195
BURST CITY   **191**, 191

C

CAGE, THE   207
CAISSON   207
CAPTURED FOR SEX 2   73–75, **74**
CAREER OF LUST   60
CARNIVAL OF NIGHT   189, **190**, 208
CATCH, THE   59
CATERPILLAR   198, 202
CATOLOGY   207
CEREMONY, THE   **59**, 59
CHARGE! LOLITA POACHING   140, 140, **141**
CHRONICLE OF A LONG WHITE LINE   207
CLOSE-UP TORTURE   75
CONCUBINE PALACE   90
CONCUBINES   63
CONSPIRACY OF THE YAGYU CLAN   91
CONVENT OF THE SACRED BEAST   32
CRAZY FAMILY   209
CRAZED FRUIT   26
CRAZY THUNDER ROAD   184, 190, **191**, 208
CREAM LEMON   102
CRIMINAL WOMEN   68, 69
CRIMINAL WOMEN REPORT: EDO INQUISITION TORTURE   70

CRUEL POST-WAR STORIES 28
CRUEL STORY OF YOUTH 59
CRUELTY OF THE FEMALE INQUISITION 70
CYCLOPS 152

D

DARK HAIR: VELVET SOUL 25
DARK STREETS 61
DAYDREAM (1964) 7, 8, 26, 28, 35
DAYDREAM (1981) 28
DAYDREAM 2 28
DEAD HORIZON 62
DEATH BY HANGING 59
DEATH FILES 165
DEATH OF A MADMAN 63, 63
DEATH OF HONOUR 93
DEATH POWDER 160, 164, **197**, 197
DEATH WOMEN 154, 155–157, **156**
DELINQUENT BOSS **177**, 177, 184
DELINQUENTS, THE 207
DEMON OF VENGEANCE 63
DESERTED REEF, THE 62, **188**, 18
DESIRES OF THE FLESH 63
DESTROY ALL MONSTERS 161
DETONATION! VIOLENT RIDERS 184
DEVIL MAN 102
DEVIL'S TEMPLE 27, 182
DEVOURED MAN, THE 189
DIARY OF A MAD OLD MAN 27
DIARY OF A SHINJUKU THIEF 3, 59, 62
DO IT AGAIN LIKE AN ANIMAL 15
DOUBLE BED 15
DOUBLE SUICIDE 3
DREAM DEVIL 75, 75, 95
DREAM OF GARUDA, THE 25
DREAM OF THE RED ROOM 28
DREAMY EXPRESS ZONE 102
DUCK SONG CONTEST 179
DUNES 188

E

ECSTASY OF WHITE FINGERS 15
ELECTRIC BIBLE: SISTER HUNTING 32
ELEGY TO VIOLENCE 14
EMBRYO HUNTS IN SECRET, THE 34, 37, 37–39, **38**, **39**, 40, 55, 60, 63
EMPEROR TOMATO KETCHUP **61**, 62, 188
EMPIRE OF PASSION 60

ENTRAILS OF A BEAUTY	164
ENTRAILS OF A VIRGIN	153–154, 164
EROS ETERNAL	**54**, 54
EROS + MASSACRE	28, 29
EROS SCHEDULE BOOK: CONCUBINE SECRETS	90
EROTIC SEDUCTION: FLESH BONDAGE	22
EROTIC SISTERS	31
EVANGELION	178
EVE IS GETTING WET	15
EVERYTHING IS CRAZY	29
EVIL DEAD TRAP	152–153, **153**
EVIL DEAD TRAP 2: HIDEKI	153
EVIL DEAD TRAP 3: BROKEN LOVE KILLER	153
EXCITING EROS: HOT SKIN	123, **124**
EXECUTIONER	94
EXORSISTER	102, 169, **170**, **182**, 182
EXORSISTER: BITCH WITH 1,000 FACES	182
EXORSISTER: DEMON SCHOOL	182
EXORSISTER: REBIRTH OF THE GREAT LUST GOD	182
EXORSISTER: WHITE UNIFORM HELL	182

54 NUDE HONEYS	169
FACE OF ANOTHER, THE	**162**, 162
FAIRY IN A CAGE	22, 31
FAMILY GAMES	189
FAT MAN AND THE OCTOPUS	208
FEMALE BONDAGE TORTURE	22
FEMALE HELL: WET FOREST	15, 63
FEMALE INQUISITOR	164
FEMALE NEO-NINJAS	99
FEMALE NINJAS: MAGIC CHRONICLES III: SACRED BOOK OF SEXUAL POSITIONS	99
FEMALE TEACHER	15
FILM	189
FILTHY TRAP	60
FILTHY VIRGIN	15
FINAL ATROCITY	151, 152
FIRST LOVE INFERNO	28
FIVE	102
FLESH MARKET	26
FLESH MEAT DOLL	75
FLOWER AND SNAKE	22, 30, **97**, 97
FLOWER OF SUMO WOMAN	169, **175**
FLOWERS IN THE SAND	26
FREE FLESH TRADE	26
FROM 1 TO 60 SECONDS	188
FRUITS OF PASSION, THE	**62**, 62
FUDOH	93
FUNERAL	184
FUNERAL PROCESSION OF ROSES	3, **119**, 119, 188, 207

GAMERA	179, 184
GAMERA, GUARDIAN OF THE UNIVERSE	184
GAMERA 2: ADVENT OF LEGION	184
GAMES OF BITCHES, THE	59
GATE OF FLESH	14, 14, 29, 68
GERRORIST	198, 202
GHIDRAH	161
GHOST CAT OF THE HAUNTED SWAMP	164
GHOST IN THE SHELL	99
GHOST OF THE HUNCHBACK	162
GHOST OF THE ONE-EYED MAN	162
GHOST STORY OF KASANE SWAMP	162
GHOST STORY OF SEX	164
GHOST STORY OF YOTSUYA	162
GIRL COP	99
GIRL IN THE FREAK-SHOW	100
GIRL LIKE MONROE, A	26
GIRLS, GIRLS, GIRLS	26
GO, GO, SECOND TIME VIRGIN	37, 44–46, **45**, **46**, 51, **52**, **53**, 55, 58
GOD SPEED YOU: BLACK EMPEROR!	184
GODZILLA	161, 179, 184
GOKE, BODY SNATCHER FROM HELL	161
GOODBYE CEREBRAL PALSY	189
GREAT BODHISATTVA PASS	172
GREAT BODHISATTVA PASS (1935)	183
GREAT BODHISATTVA PASS II (1936)	183
GREAT BODHISATTVA PASS (1957)	183
GREAT BODHISATTVA PASS II (1958)	183
GREAT BODHISATTVA PASS III (1958)	183
GROTESQUE PERVERTED SLAUGHTER	72
GUINEA PIG	150, 151, 152, 198
GUINEA PIG: DEVIL'S EXPERIMENT	145–149, **146**, **148**, 158, 160
GUINEA PIG 2: FLOWER OF BLOODY FLESH	141, 142, 146, **149**, **150**, 158–159, **159**, 160
GUINEA PIG 2: ANDROID OF NOTRE DAME	160
GUINEA PIG 4: MERMAID IN A MANHOLE	**160**, 160
GUINEA PIG 5: DEVIL WOMAN DOCTOR	119
GUZOO	102

H-MAN	161
HAIRY PISTOL	3
HALF HUMAN	192
HALF-NAKED REAL TAKE: RAPING FEMALE UNIVERSITY STUDENTS	124, **128**
HALO OF HEAT HAZE	182
HANZO THE BLADE	84, 91, 93
HARD FOCUS: WIRETAPPING	123, **127**

HAUNTED CASTLE, THE	164
HAUNTED HOUSE OF AMA	88
HEATWAVE ISLAND	28
HELL	162
HELL SCREEN	164
HEX	189
HIDDEN FILMING REPORT: SNEAK SHOTS see: Turtle Vision	
HIDDEN FORTRESS, THE	94
HIGH-HEELED PUNISHERS	102
HIGH SCHOOL BIG PANIC	208
HIROKU: MONSTER HUNTING	209
HISTORY OF TORTURE AND PUNISHMENT	68, 97
HOPSCOTCH	188
HORNY MARRIED WOMAN: WET	123, 131
HORROR OF A MALFORMED MAN	89, 95
HORSE, WOMAN, DOG	140
HOT SPRINGS GEISHA	177
HOUSE	164, 189
HUMAN CHAIR	96
HUNGRY SEX BEAST	97

I

I'LL RAPE YOU WHENEVER I WANT	72
I WILL GROPE YOU	15
IDIOT IN LOVE	27
IKO, EARTH DEFENDER	178
INDUSTRY AND THE SEX DOLL	208
INFERNO	164
INFLATABLE SEX DOLL OF THE WASTELANDS	60
INSATIABLE	32
ISLAND	95
IT'S A WOMAN'S WORLD	28

J

JAPAN 69: SEX ZONE	165
JAPAN BY NIGHT	165
JOY GIRLS	29
JOY OF TORTURE 2	90, 183
JOY STREET	15
JOYS OF TORTURE, THE	68–70, 89
JUNK FOOD	208, 208–209

K

KALEIDOSCOPE: TORTURE OF BEAUTIFUL FLESH	140

KEKKO MASK   184
KEKKO MASK IN LOVE   184
KEKKO MASK: THE MOVIE   99, 178, 184
KEY, THE (1959)   27
KEY, THE (1974)   27, 27
KEY, THE (1998)   32
KIKUCHI   195
KINGDOM, THE   62
KURONEKO   95, 162–163, 163
KWAIDAN   120, 162, 163
KYOKO NAKAMURA IN BONDAGE   81
KYOSHIRO NEMURI: FLAMING SWORD   182
KYOSHIRO NEMURI: SON OF THE BLACK MASS   91, 172, 182, 183

L

LABYRINTH OF DREAMS   209, 209
LADY SNOWBLOOD   91
LADY TAX OFFICER   184
LAST FRANKENSTEIN   62
LEATHER STRAPS AND YUKI   75
LEGEND OF WOLVES   170
LEGENDARY PANTY MASK   99
LEND A CHILD, LEND AN ARM   91, 182
LESBIAN RAPE: SWEET SYRUP   85
LET ME DIE FOR TEN SECONDS   15
LIGHTNING SWORDS OF DEATH   93
LIVE ACT: TOP STRIPPER   15
LIVE BUGGING REPORT: DIRTY TALK   140
LOLITA: VIBRATOR TORTURE   123, 126, 145, 145
LONE WOLF   183
LONE WOLF COP   93
LONE WOLF WITH CUB   91, 93, 171, 177
LOST PARADISE   154–155, 155
LOST SEX   95
LOVE   188
LOVE HUNTER   15, 22
LOVE HUNTER: HOT SKIN   15
LOVE ROBOTS, THE   60
LOVERS ARE WET   30
LOYAL 47 RONIN, THE   119
LUCKY STAR DIAMOND   150
LUSTY DIVER   89

M

MAD LOVE   15
MAD MASTURBATOR IN A GASMASK   81
MALE KILLER, FEMALE KILLER, NAKED BULLET   63

MAN WITH THE EMBOSSED TAPESTRY 96
MANDALA 3
MANIAC RAPIST WITH HANDCUFFS: TORMENT! 85, **86**
MARRIED WOMAN COLLECTOR 124, **125**, 140
MARRIED WOMAN: PERVERT HAIRDRESSER 123, **131**
MARTIAL LAW **118**, 118
MASTURBATION IN UNIFORM: VIRGINS' PANTIES 123, **130**
MATANGO **161**, 161
MEIJI, TAISHO AND SHOWA ERA: GROTESQUE CRUELTY TO WOMEN 70
MEMOIRS OF A CAPTURED GIRL 75
MERMAID LEGEND 102
MINI-SKIRT COPS L.E.G.S. 169
MODERN SEX CRIMES: CONFESSIONS OF A DEMON KILLER 63
MODERN SEX CRIMES: FIERCE SCREAMS, WILD RAPE 63
MOJU 76, 76–79, **77**, **78**, **79**, 95
MONSTERS ON CAMPUS 102
MOTHER 189
MOTHRA 161
MY PRIVATE EROS: LOVE SONG **189**, 189

N

NAKED BLOOD 136–139, **136**, **137**, **138**, 141–142, 145
NAKED ISLAND 26
NAKED SHADOW, THE 59
NAMU 188
NAOMI SUGISHITA IN BONDAGE 81
NARCISSUS OF LUST 60
NASTY DIVER 89
NEJISHIKI 179
NIGHT AND FOG IN JAPAN 59
NIGHT IN THE NUDE, A 102
NIGHT LADIES 26
NIGHT OF THE SHE-CATS 15
NIGHTY NIGHT 152
NOISY REQUIEM **187**, 187, 192–193, **193**
NUBILE SEX SLAVES 75
NUDE 189
NUDE GIRL WITH A GUN 88
NURSE'S JOURNAL: NASTY FILE 15, 30

O

OH MY MOTHER 188
ONE HUNDRED MONSTERS 164
ONIBABA 3, **71**, 71–72, **72**, 95, 162
ORGAN 62, 93, **197**, **198**, 198, 202
ORGIES OF EDO **69**, 70
ORGY 61

ORGY OF KILLING   75
ORIGINAL SIN   102
OSTIA: LUNAR ECLIPSE CINEMA   140

P|Q

PAGES OF MADNESS   187
PAINFUL BLISS! FINAL TWIST   15
PALE FLOWER   29
PANDEMONIUM   119–120, 207, 207
PASSION   27
PEEP SHOW   188
PERVERT AND PEEPING TOM: GYNAECOLOGY WARD   123
PIG-CHICKEN-SUICIDE   192, 192
PINK CURTAIN   15
PINOCCHIO 964   160, 198–200, 199, 202, 206
PITFALL   161
PLASTIC MODEL IN THE NIGHT   208
PLAYGIRLS   169
PLAYGIRLS 2   169, 174
PLEASE RAPE ME AGAIN   84
PLEASURES OF THE FLESH   59
POOL WITHOUT WATER   53, 84
PORNO QUEEN: JAPANESE SEX TRIP   165
PORNO SAMURAI THEATRE: BOHACHI CODE OF HONOUR   70
PORNOGRAPHERS   28
POSI-?   189
PREDATOR'S DIARY, A   26
PRIVATE TORTURE OF UNIFORMS: THRUST IT IN!   124, 129
PUNISHMENT ROOM   26, 26

R

RAMPO   96
RAN   119
RAPE!!   81, 81
RAPE: CLIMAX   124, 125
RAPE: FOR REAL   123, 126
RAPE OF OFFICE LADIES   85, 85
RAPE TRAP   61
RAPED IN HEAVEN: BEAUTIFUL HUMILIATION   84
RAPEMAN   85–87, 178
RASHOMON   94
RAZOR HANZO'S TORTURE HELL   93
REBEL, THE   59
RED ANGEL   95, 95
RED ARMY PFLP: WORLD WAR STATEMENT   64
RED CRIME   59
RETURN OF MAJIN   182

REVENGE OF THE PEARL QUEEN 88
RHETORIC OF CELLOPHANE, THE 189
RIKKI O 94
RITUAL OF LOVE AND DEATH 118, 118
ROAMING TORTURED BRAIN 84
RODAN 161
ROLLA 62
ROPE AND BREASTS 22, 30
ROPE AND SKIN 97
ROPE HUNT 75
ROPE SLAVE 22, 31
ROSE DANCE 188
ROSEBUD 188
RUBBER LADY 75
RUBBER'S LOVER 160, **200**, 200–202, **201**, **203**, 204, 205
RUINED MAP, THE 161

S

S/M 73
SADISTIC VIOLENCE TO TEN VIRGINS 75
SANJURO 94
SATAN'S SWORD 183
SAVAGE WOMEN 59
SAYURI ICHIJO'S WET LUST 15
SCENT OF THE WILDCAT 31
SCHOOL MISTRESS 15
SCHOOLGIRL GUERILLA 60
SCORE 93
SCORPION: FEMALE PRISONER 70
SCREAMING FLESH TARGET 63
SEASON OF TERROR 55, **56**
SEASON OF TREASON 60
SEASON OF VIOLENCE 26
SECRET ACTS WITHIN FOUR WALLS 35, **36**
SECRET CHRONICLE: PROSTITUTE TORTURE HELL 15
SECRET CHRONICLE: SHE-BEAST MARKET 15
SECRET LIFE OF SHOGUN 170, **171**
SECRET REPORT FROM A WOMEN'S PRISON 68, 68
SECRET REPORT FROM NAGASAKI WOMEN'S PRISON 70
SECRETS OF A WOMEN'S TEMPLE 32
SENSUAL BEASTS 97
SEPPUKU 71
SERIAL RAPE OF OFFICE LADIES: DEVOUR BIG TITS 85, **86**
SERIAL RAPE OF SISTERS: GOUGE IT OUT! 85
SERIAL RAPE: PERVERSION EXPERIMENTS 85, **87**
SEVEN DAYS OF TORTURE 75
SEVEN SAMURAI, THE 90, 94
SEX BEAST 61
SEX BEAST ON CAMPUS 102
SEX BEAST TEACHER 102

SEX CRIMES   61
SEX DOCUMENTARY: STUDENT WORLD   165
SEX GAMES   60
SEX IN CHAINS   75
SEX JACK   49, 50, 56, 56
SEX VIRGIN TEAM: BANQUET OF BEASTS   140
SEX-CRAZED DAIMYO, THE   90, 165
SEXUAL ABUSE   73
SHAMELESS: ABNORMAL AND ABUSIVE LOVE   70
SHINJUKU MAD   49, 50, 57
SHITSURAKU-EN   165
SHOCKS, THE   165, 165
SHOGUN ASSASSIN   171, 182
SHOJO GEBA GEBA   37, 46–49, 47, 48, 53, 60
SHOOT AND WET   30
SKY   189
SLAVE WIFE   22
SMILE   188
SNAKE LUST   164
SONGS OF MALDOROR, THE   62
SONS, THE   188
SPECIAL LESSON: PERVERTED SEX EDUCATION   123, 129
SPIDER GIRL   27, 27, 95
SPIRAL ZONE   169, 173, 183
SPOTS IN THE SUN   165
SQUAREWORLD   194
STAR OF DAVID: BEAUTY HUNTING   32, 84
STONE, A   188
STORIES FROM THE UNDERGROUND HISTORY OF JAPANESE SEX VIOLENCE   61
STREETFIGHTER   93–94
SUGATA SANSHIRO   94
SUKEBAN DEKA   99
SUN'S BURIAL, THE   59
SUZAKI PARADISE   204, 210
SWEET HOME   164
SWEET TRAP   59
SWORD OF DOOM   183

T

TALE OF GENJI, THE   28
TALE OF MOON   188
TALES OF SACRED HUMILIATION   25
TALES OF THE PALE MOON AFTER RAIN   162, 184
TAMPOPO   184
TANDEM   25, 25
TASTIEST FLESH   152
TATTOOED FOR TORTURE   75
TATTOOED WOMAN, THE   188
TEN YEARS OF EVIL   72
TETSUO   3, 62, 152, 160, 160, 195, 195, 196, 197, 198, 200, 202

TETSUO 2 – BODY HAMMER   195–196
THIRD SHADOW   183
THOUGHT BEAST, THE   189
THREE DAYS OF SUB-HUMAN TREATMENT   75
THRONE OF BLOOD   120, 120
THROW AWAY YOUR BOOKS AND GO OUT   3
TO BECOME BLIND IN THE RIGHT EYE   207
TOKUGAWA TATTOO HISTORY: TORTURE HELL   70
TOKUGAWA WOMEN BLOODLINE   70, 177
TOKYO CRASH   **194**, 194
TOKYO DRIFTER   14, 175, **183**, 183–184
TOKYO FIST   209, **210**
TOPAZ   25
TORN LUST   60
TORTURE CHRONICLES: 100 YEARS   70
TORTURE CHRONICLES CONTINUES   70
TORTURE OF MARRIED WOMEN: THE THREE STEPS   123, **130**
TOWN OF LOVE AND HOPE, A   29, 59
TRAIN OF PERVERSION: DIRTY ACTIONS   124
TREAD LIGHTLY ON THE ROAD TO HELL   93
TRUE STORY OF A WOMAN CONDEMNED   70
TRUE STORY OF SADA ABE, THE   116, 116
TURTLE VISION   **132**, 132–133

U

ULTRAMAN   161
UNDER THE CHERRY BLOSSOMS   164
UNDERGROUND HISTORY OF JAPANESE SEX VIOLENCE: BLOOD OF A STRANGER 61
UNDERGROUND HISTORY OF JAPANESE SEX VIOLENCE: RAGING BEAST   61
UNDERGROUND HISTORY OF JAPANESE SEX VIOLENCE 2: RANK OPPRESSIVE EVIL 61
UNFAITHFUL WIFE: SHAMEFUL TORTURE see: Bedroom, The
UNIFORM GIRLS: THE FRUIT IS RIPE   15
UNO KOICHIRO'S NURSES' JOURNAL   23
UP AND WET   30

V

VALLEY OF CARNAL DESIRES   89
VARAN   161
VICIOUS DOCTOR   72
VIOLATED ANGELS   30, 37, 40–44, **41**, **42**, **43**, **44**, 45, 46, 47, 53, 54, 56, 61, 63
VIOLATED NUN   177
VIOLENCE AT NOON   59
VIOLENT COP   93, **94**
VIOLENT VIRGIN see: Shojo Geba Geba
VIRGIN CRUELTY   72

WALKER IN THE ATTIC   95, **96**
WALKERS ON THE TIGER'S TAIL   119
WANDERING KID   100–102, **101**
WAR OF THE 16-YEAR-OLDS   207
WATCHDOGS FROM HELL   99
WET BUNDLE   30
WET COMEHOMING   30
WET LIPS   15
WET LUST: OPEN TULIP   15
WET ROPE CONFESSION   30, **30**
WET SAND IN AUGUST   30
WET WEEKEND   30
WHITE BABY DOLL   60
WHITE SKIN IN THE DARK   72, **73**
WHITE UNIFORM STORY: RAPE!   15, 30
WICKED PRIEST   91
WIDOW IN MOURNING: SHAVEN ROPE BITCH   123
WIDOW IN PERVERT HELL   123
WIFE TO BE SACRIFICED   22, 30
WIFE'S SEXUAL FANTASY: BEFORE HUSBAND'S EYES   15
WILD BEAST   204
WILD BEAST OF YOUTH   14
WIZARD OF DARKNESS   99
WOMAN ABUSE: NAKED BLOOD see: Naked Blood
WOMAN I ABANDONED, THE   207
WOMAN IN THE BOX: VIRGIN SACRIFICE   22
WOMAN OF THE DUNES   161
WOMAN WITH RED HAIR, THE   15, 60
WOMAN'S TRAIL: WET PATH   30
WOMB TO LET   63
WOMEN IN HEAT BEHIND BARS   15
WOMEN, OH! WOMEN   28
WORLD APARTMENT HORROR   **193**, 194

XX: BEAUTIFUL WEAPON   164

YAKUZA TORTURE HISTORY: LYNCHING!   68
YOJIMBO   71, 90, **91**
YUKA ON MONDAY   26

ZATOICHI: BLIND SWORDSMAN   91, 92, 177, 182
ZATOICHI'S BLOODY PATH   182
ZERO WOMAN   84
ZIPANG   91
ZOOM-UP   15

ACCUSED, THE	102
BAD TASTE	210
BATMAN	178
BEAST, THE	164
BEYOND ULTRA VIOLENCE – UNEASY LISTENING BY MERZBOW	164
BLACK MAGIC 2	164
BLOOD OF DR JEKYLL	164
BRAIN THAT WOULDN'T DIE, THE	28
BRAINDEAD	210
CLOCKWORK ORANGE, A	60
CRASH	142
DEAD RINGERS	142
ENTER THE DRAGON	180
EVIL DEAD	164
FACES OF DEATH	155
FASTER, PUSSYCAT, GO! GO!	60
FISTFUL OF DOLLARS, A	90
FORCED ENTRY	96
FREAKS	100
HALLOWEEN	164
HAUNTING, THE	164
I WANT MORE	96
INAUGURATION OF THE PLEASURE DOME	37
LADY FROM SHANGHAI, THE	180
LORNA	60
MAD MAX	208
MAGNIFICENT SEVEN, THE	90
MERRY CHRISTMAS, MR LAWRENCE	60
MOTORPSYCHO!	60
MUDHONEY	60
ORGY OF THE DEAD	172
PLAN NINE FROM OUTER SPACE	172
POSSESSION	205
SALO	49, 63–64
SEEDING OF A GHOST	164
STAR WARS	155
TEXAS CHAINSAW MASSACRE	205
UN CHIEN ANDALOU	37
VIDEODROME	142
WATERPOWER	96

Directors are listed alphabetically by family name, followed by first name as in Japan. This index includes full entries for actors, writers etc who have also made one or more film.

Adachi Masao	60, 64, 187
Akita Masami	67, 80, 154, 155, 164, 165
Akiyama Tomo	184
Akutagawa Katsuo	26
Ando Kohei	188
Aoyama Sadaji	205
Fujita Toshiya	15, 30
Fujiura Atsushi	89
Fujiwara Kei	62, 93, 197, 198, 202
Fukasaku Kinji	3, 90–91, 93, 176, 179, 184
Fukui Shojin	160, 198, 199, 200, 202–206
Go Ijuin	73, 74, 75
Gosha Hideo	90
Hagiwara Sakumi	189
Hani Susumu	28, 187
Hara Kazuo	189
Hara Masato	189
Harada Hiroshi	100
Hasebe Yasuharu	15, 81
Hashimoto Izo	150, 153
Hattori Mitsunori	102
Hayashi Isao	90
Hayashi Kaizo	91
Higashi Yoichi	188
Hino Hideshi	149, 158, 160
Hiroki Ryuichi	73, 75
Honda Inoshiro	161
Ichikawa Kon	26–27, 119
Iimura Taka	188
Ikeda Toshiharu	32, 102, 152, 153
Imamura Shohei	28, 187
Inagaki Hiroshi	183
Inoue Akira	67, 68
Inoue Shinsuke	84
Inoue Umeji	184
Ishii Sogo	184, 190, 191, 192, 195, 208, 209
Ishii Takashi	84, 89, 102
Ishii Teruo	68, 69, 71, 89, 164, 172, 177, 179, 184
Ishikawa Hitoshi	73, 75
Ishikawa Yoshihiro	164
Itami Juzo	179, 184
Iwamoto Kenichi	195
Iwasa Hisaya	188
Izumiya Shigeru	160, 164, 197
Jissoji Akio	3
i Takehiko	188
	62, 188
	184
	188
	53, 62
	99

Kato Akira	15
Kawabe Kazuo	207
Kawamura Takeshi	62
Kawasaki Minoru	178
Kawashima Yuzo	205, 210
Kimura Keigo	27
Kinugasa Teinosuke	119, 187
Kobayashi Kaname	102
Kobayashi Masaki	71, 72, 90, 162, 163
Kobayashi Satoru	26
Kobayashi Tsuneo	162
Komizu Kazuo ("Gaira")	153, 164, 173, 187
Komori Baku	68, 97, 164
Komoto Kyoichi	194
Konuma Masaru	15, 22, 30, 97
Kumai Kei	207
Kumashiro Tatsumi	15, 27, 60, 63, 164
Kurata Takeo	26
Kuroki Kazuo	188
Kurosawa Akira	71, 90, 91, 94, 119, 120, 187, 205
Kurosawa Kiyoshi	164
Magatani Morihei	71
Makamura Genji	73, 75
Makiguchi Yuji	90
Masumura Yasuzo	27, 76, 77, 79, 93, 95, 187
Matsui Yoshihiko	187, 192, 195
Matsumoto Toshio	3, 119, 188, 207
Matsumoto Yoji	102
Matsumura Katsuya	150, 151
Miike Takashi	93
Mishima Yukio	118, 176
Misumi Kenji	27, 91, 92, 93, 172, 182, 183
Miyagawa Takayuki	184
Mizoguchi Kenji	162, 177, 184
Morita Yoshimitsu	189
Murakami Ryu	25
Murakawa Toru	15
Muroga Atsushi	93
Nagaishi Takao	85
Naito Makoto	184
Nakagawa Nobuo	120, 162, 165
Nakahira Ko	26
Nakajima Sadao	165
Nakano Takao	102, 169–184
Negishi Kichitaro	15
Nishihara Giishi	72, 84, 164
Nishimura Shogoro	15
Noda Yukio	177, 184
Nureki Chimuo	79, 80, 165
Obayashi Nobuhiko	164, 188–189
Ogawa Shinsuke	188

Ohara Koya 70
Ohno Kelzo 165
Ohta Akikazu 70
Okabe Michio 189
Okamoto Kihachi 90, 183
Okishima Isao 188
Okumura Teruo 189
Okuyama Kazuyoshi 95
Onishi Kenji 194, 195
Oshii Mamoru 99
Oshima Nagisa 3, 29, 35, 51, 59–60, 62, 76, 105, 106, 108, 109, 111, 112, 114, 115, 116, 117, 164, 187, 190
Otomo Katsuhiro 193, 194
Ozawa Shigehiro 93
Ozu Yasujiro 187
Sano Kazuhiro 123, 173
Saruyama Norichio 208
Sato Hajime 161, 162
Sato Hisayasu 85, 86, 87, 123–142, 145, 173
Sato Mitsumasa 91
Sato Shimako 99, 100
Sato Takemitsu 93
Satoh Toshiki 25, 123, 173
Seki Koji 89
Sekimoto Ikuo 90
Shibuya Minoru 26
Shindo Kaneto 28, 71, 72, 95, 162, 163
Shinoda Masahiro 3, 29, 164, 187
Shirao Kazuhiro 208
Suzuki Norifumi 32, 84, 90, 165
Suzuki Seijun 14, 15, 29, 35, 67, 88, 175, 184, 187
Takabayashi Yoichi 188
Takayama Hideki 100, 101
Takechi Tetsuji 7, 8, 28, 35
Takeshi Beat 93, 94
Tanaka Hideo 99
Tanaka Noboru 15, 95, 96, 116
Tanaka Tokizo 164
Tani Naomi 15, 81, 97
Terayama Shuji 3, 62, 188, 207
Teshigahara Hiroshi 161, 162, 187
Toyoda Shiro 164
Tsuchimoto Noriaki 188
Tsukamoto Shinya 152, 160, 192, 195, 196, 197, 209, 210
Tsushima Masaru 70, 99
Uchida Kentaro 165
Uchida Tomu 183
Urayama Kiriro 207
Wakamatsu Koji 14, 28, 30, 35–62, 67, 70, 84, 123, 173, 187, 190
Yamaguchi Seiichiro 22
Yamamoto Masashi 189, 190, 192, 193, 208
Yamamoto Shinya 70
Yamashita Osamu 188
Yamatoya Atsushi 3, 60, 63, 187

Yanagimachi Mitsuo 184
Yasuda Kimiyoshi 164
Yoshida Yoshishige 28, 118
Yoshimura Kimisaburo 119
Zeke Takahisa 25, 123, 173